Getting Closer to Japan
Getting Along with the Japanese

Getting
Along
with the Japanese

Kate Elwood

ASK Co., Ltd.
Tokyo, Japan

Getting Closer to Japan

Getting Along with the Japanese

Copyright © 2001   by Kate Elwood
Published in Japan by ASK Co., Ltd.
All rights reserved.

Book design by   Masami Jimbo
Illustrations by   Mika Omori
Editing by   Yoko Otsuka, Hiroko Kageyama, and Masako Iijima
Proofreading by   Chris Cataldo
Supervised by   Prof. Kaoru Kobayashi (Sanno University)
DTP and printing by   SHINANO CO., LTD.
ISBN 4-87217-065-2
Getting Along with the Japanese

The information included is available as of February 2001.
The publisher cannot be responsible for any subsequent changes in said infomation.
First edition, March 2001

Printed in Japan

Contents

Foreword   7

Section 1 *Twelve Key Words Useful in Understanding the Japanese*

Inside and Outside ·· *10*
Group Harmony ··· *12*
Real Intentions and Stated Principles ··············· *14*
Shame ·· *16*
Inference ··· *18*
Ambiguity ·· *20*
Diligence ··· *22*
Perseverance ·· *24*
Consideration for Others ································· *26*
Bullying ·· *28*
Moral Obligation·· *30*
Modesty ·· *32*

Section 2 *Face to Face with the Japanese*

Meeting Someone for the First Time ················ *36*
Hellos and Goodbyes ······································ *38*
What to Call People ·· *40*
Nonverbal Communication ······························ *42*
Expressing Gratitude·· *44*
Apologizing ·· *46*
Complimenting·· *48*
Invitations ·· *50*
Requests ·· *52*
Age Differences ··· *54*
Getting Along with Friends ······························ *56*

Getting Along with Neighbors ·· *58*

Going Out to Eat ··· *60*

Gift-Giving Seasons ·· *62*

Gifts for Special Occasions ·· *64*

Greeting Cards ··· *66*

Visiting Others' Homes ·· *68*

Eating at People's Homes ·· *70*

Going Out Drinking ·· *72*

Really, Really Good to Know ·· *74*

Section 3 *Important Life Events*

Meeting Someone and Getting Engaged ······························ *78*

Weddings ··· *80*

Wedding Q&A ·· *82*

Age-Related Events ·· *84*

New Year's ·· *86*

Death ··· *88*

Funeral Q&A ··· *90*

Other Beginnings and Endings ··· *92*

Index ··· *94*

Foreword

Many people who have come to live in Japan for periods of varying length have confessed to me that for at least the first few years they often found themselves in situations where they didn't really understand what was going on. Part of this was a linguistic problem, but more often the uncertainty had its base in cultural differences. Even if a simultaneous interpreter had been available throughout their stay there still would have been frequent occasions of confusion.

As guests to Japan, you don't want to unintentionally offend anyone, yet you soon realize that many of the rules of the game are quite different. Sometimes the game itself is different: you're playing basketball on a tennis court. When the differences are explicit, for example, chopsticks vs. forks, it's easy to see what's going on. But the subtler the differences are, the more likely you are to find yourself in situations where you feel some kind of gap, something that is lost in the translation.

The Japanese are not being churlish in not explaining their culture fully: they are often unaware that certain things that seem like commonsense are far from it to the beleaguered foreigner. The explanations are not forthcoming because no one realizes that there is a need for explanations. And you don't know the right questions to ask because all your questions are based on your own cultural context. A question related to basketball probably won't help you a bit when playing tennis.

When I tell Japanese people about the kinds of situations many foreign people I know, myself included, have been puzzled or taken aback by, they are often astonished that such normal situations could cause bewilderment. This is true even if the person speaks English well.

This book is designed to help you become aware of some of the less obvious differences between Japan and the West. It is my hope that the information provided piques your interest in Japanese everyday business culture and serves as a roadmap when you feel lost in a cultural fog.

The book is divided into three parts. Section 1, "Twelve Key Words Useful in Understanding the Japanese" addresses Japanese values within the framework of situations that foreign businesspeople living in Japan are likely to encounter. Each essay answers the question "Why do the Japanese behave the way they do here?" through a look at the answer to the question "What is important to the Japanese?"

The concepts explained in Section 1 form a background for the general situations described in Section 2, "Face to Face with the Japanese." This section shows how various values find their concrete reflection in the way Japanese people accomplish many ordinary social functions and has more of a how-to approach than the first, somewhat more theoretical, section.

The final section, "Important Life Events," deals with occasions that people don't usually encounter on a daily basis but which are special and more ritualized. You may not participate in some of these events, but after reading the book, when you witness any one of them you will be able to think "Oh, that's what's going on!"

For others, such as weddings and funerals, it is highly likely that if you live in Japan you will have the opportunity to join in the observance of these momentous occasions, which will be more meaningful to you because of your deeper understanding.

My biggest difficulty in writing the book was a reluctance to describe the Japanese categorically. There are many types of Japanese people and, especially recently, values are changing and diversifying rapidly. On the other hand, even if one Japanese person's values or actions might not necessarily be the same as another Japanese person's, they usually can read each other, or understand what's going on much better than a non-Japanese person. There is a strong, shared body of cultural knowledge. Rather than saying "All Japanese people ..." it is more a matter of saying, "No Japanese people are surprised by ..."

The process of writing the book engendered many lively discussions between me and my Japanese editors as well as many of my other Japanese and non-Japanese friends and colleagues. After living in Japan for 18 years and speaking Japanese fluently, I thought nothing would catch me unawares but tackling a book like this led to many new insights.

Japanese colleagues and friends who I consulted while writing the book agreed with my interpretations and explanations. The book does not represent all of Japan's complexity but I am confident that what is represented is accurate and useful. This is the book that I wish I had read before coming to Japan.

Kate Elwood
February, 2001
Tokyo, Japan

Twelve Key Words
Useful in
Understanding the Japanese

Inside and Outside

Will I ever be an insider?

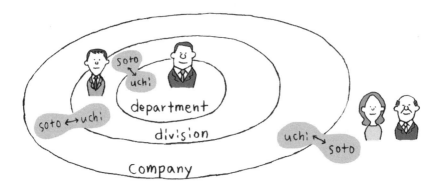

Steve Wilson began work in Japan three years ago. He enjoys his work and finds his colleagues helpful and kind. However, it's been three years and Steve wonders why he still seems to be kept at a slight distance. Japanese employees who joined the company after him seemed to quickly enjoy a more relaxed relationship with everyone.

Gaijin

When considering Japan's attitude to foreigners it is important to recall that Japan was a country closed to foreigners for more than 200 years until Commodore Perry arrived with his black ships in 1853 and reopened the country. Today there are many foreigners in Japan, but the "us and them" mentality lingers on.

The most widely used term for foreigners is *gaijin*, which literally means "outside person." **Most Japanese people see the word *gaijin* as descriptive rather than pejorative.** However, many foreigners in Japan view it as a putdown. The problem is not the word itself but that the assessment "outside person" is applied so automatically and immediately without considering what country the person is from, what kind of work they do, or anything else.

Other outsiders

Being a foreigner is undoubtedly the biggest distinction that Japanese make between outsiders and insiders. However, the *uchi* (inside) and *soto* (outside) differentiation is made at many levels among Japanese themselves. **The two most basic groups of insiders are those belonging to the same family and those belonging to the same company.**

If a woman says *uchi no hito* (the inside person) she means her husband. Company employees also refer to other employees using expressions that mean "inside person": *uchi no ningen* or *naibu no hito*. People outside the company are *gaibu no hito*.

However, there are other ways to cut the *uchi/soto* pie: for example, those who attended the same university, belong to the same club, or are on the same neighborhood committee.

These insider/outsider distinctions are like the rings of a tree, with circle upon circle. **Within a company, the department is one circle within the circle of the company itself.** In turn, the company is part of a network of other companies that consider themselves insiders in relation to other companies and so on.

Finding a way in

You'll always be a foreigner but it is possible to build relationships with Japanese people who see you as much more than simply someone from another country.

If you want to feel more included, here are three pieces of advice. **First, try to find someone in your company who speaks English or any other language, and/or has lived abroad.** Such colleagues are usually more accessible and once you become close to them their friends will slowly open up as well.

Secondly, try to speak at least a little Japanese. Don't worry if it's not easy to make yourself understood. The fact that you are making an effort to communicate with your Japanese colleagues in their own language is more important than the result.

Thirdly, try to never pass up an opportunity to socialize, for example, going out drinking after work. These are important chances for your colleagues to get to know you as a person, which is the goal. It may take longer than you expect, but if you make the effort, in time, some Japanese people will think of you as "one of us." You'll be in!

G o o d *to* **k n o w** ·······································

● うちのかいしゃ ［*uchi no kaisha*］　　▷ our company

● がいぶのひと ［*gaibu no hito*］　　▷ someone on the outside

● したしくなる ［*shitashiku naru*］　　▷ become friendly with

● のみにいく ［*nomi ni iku*］　　▷ go out drinking

● かおをだす ［*kao o dasu*］　　▷ put in an appearance

● なかまとしてみとめる
　［*nakama to shite mitomeru*］　　▷ recognize as an insider

● うちわ ［*uchiwa*］　　▷ people on the inside

● がいこくじん ［*gaikokujin*］　　▷ a foreigner: used on official documents and considered the politically correct term but not as widely used as *gaijin*

Group Harmony

Why don't they speak up?

Carla Nelson is surprised at how long it takes for simple decisions to be reached among her colleagues. One day when they went out to eat together it seemed like they stood outside their office building for a long time debating all the possibilities before finally settling on the chosen restaurant. She wonders why they devote so much time and energy to such trivial matters.

Wonderful *wa*

The Japanese love the idea of group harmony, or *wa*. **A sentiment often expressed by company employees regarding their goals within the company is *teki o tsukuranai*, not to make any enemies.** Put more positively, there's strength in numbers. When there's no dissent, the group stands firm and as a group it can achieve much more than each person individually.

Before anything is decided in Japan there is a period of back and forth conversation in which the views of each person are carefully and fully ascertained. The Japanese don't see this as a waste of time. To them, it's a normal way of acting to preserve the good feelings (harmony) of the group.

The conversation may seem to be going nowhere but in fact, slowly but surely, subtle hints are thrown out, often in the form of questions or indirect statements, like "Is there a possibility that ...?" or "Something to consider might be ..." and finally a consensus is reached. **Usually there is someone who will emerge as the leader, not so much by shaping the course of action as by skillfully summarizing the input of others.**

No compromises

Japanese businesspeople often claim that they never compromise: *Zettai dakyō shinai!* On the other hand, to

Westerners it often appears that the Japanese are compromising all the time in order to preserve *wa*.

What is different is the perception of what compromise entails and at what stage compromise is even possible. The word "compromise" is rarely used in reference to what goes on in discussions within a person's own group.

It is only when the group's position as a whole has solidified that compromise vis-à-vis other groups becomes an issue. **Your single opinion is not really a full-fledged opinion, it is but one ingredient that makes up the opinion or policy of the group.** Just as a carrot is not "making concessions" to a potato in the making of a stew, each vegetable has its place but none tries to overpower the others.

Once the stew is all set, it will negotiate firmly with all the other dishes on the corporate table. But the idea of an onion on its own refusing to cooperate during the food preparation stage is simply ridiculous.

When you feel strongly about something

You're already probably the most pungent ingredient so a little goes a long way. **Make sure to listen fully to everyone else's comments and don't try to speed up the process.**

Before making your suggestion it is a good idea to first mention the merits of all the choices under consideration. Then go ahead and say how you feel. If you express your opinion in a way that is palatable it will be taken into serious consideration. That's what group harmony is all about.

G o o d *to* **k n o w** ·····································

● わをまもる ［wa o mamoru］ ▷ preserving the harmony of the group
● わをみだす ［wa o midasu］ ▷ disturb the harmony of the group
● あわせる ［awaseru］ ▷ go along with (the opinion or decision of the rest)
● ごうい ［gōi］ ▷ mutual understanding, agreement
● ひととなかよくできる ▷ able to get along with others
　［hito to nakayoku dekiru］
● きがあう ［ki ga au］ ▷ feel the same way
● いけんをまとめる ［iken o matomeru］ ▷ sum up the group's position

Real Intentions and Stated Principles

Is it a lie or not?

Bill Russell and his colleague, Tsubasa Yoshida, both have children in kinder-garten. Bill knew that some Japanese children go to private elementary schools and he asked Yoshida-*san* about his plans for his son. Yoshida-*san* replied that he wasn't thinking about prestigious schools at all. But in February Bill found out that Yoshida-*san*'s son had been accepted to a prestigious school and that he had studied hard to get in. Why hadn't Yoshida-*san* told him the truth?

No betrayal of trust

What Yoshida-*san* said was *tatemae*, his stated, socially acceptable principle, as opposed to *honne*, his real intention. The written characters for *honne* mean "real sound" and those for *tatemae* derive from a building term referring to the erection of a house frame. This points to the fact that **tatemae is a construc-tion, but one which is viewed as a nec-essary support and cover.**

Why did Yoshida-*san* need this cover? Japanese people are often reluctant to reveal private hopes and ambitions. It can put them in a risky position. First of all, they may be seen as selfish and self-serving. Secondly, if they fail publicly in their ambitions they will be ashamed.

Adults in every culture know that there is sometimes a gap between what people say and what they really feel. The difference is that Japanese people expect the gap as a matter of course. Therefore, **they almost never feel betrayed if someone ends up doing something quite different from what they have stated.**

Proper *tatemae*

Japanese people do not think of *tatemae* as a lie. They see it as something vital to the smooth functioning of human relationships. **Tatemae mirrors certain values that have been decided on by a group or society at large.** Everyone knows that these values are not upheld all the time, but the appearance of these values, *tatemae*, can be.

One value in Japan is that everyone should be more or less the same, equal. This is reflected in the extremely common *tatemae* that parents have no desire for their children to go to a good private school. By saying that he had no plans for his son, Yoshida-*san* was in effect saying that he was no better than he should be, in other words, not uppity.

That people do not speak their *honne* in public is deemed proper. In fact, when people do voice their real feelings in public they are likely to add apologetically, *sore wa watashi no honne desu kedo* — "but that is my *honne*." You are only lying if you state something as *honne* that is not true.

Recognizing *honne* and *tatemae*

It is important to realize that the chances are very high that any opinion or policy stated in public has been edited. If you feel you need to know a person's true intentions you can ask him or her. However, you are unlikely to get a truthful response unless you ask in person, out of the presence of others.

The most usual way of finding out how a person really feels is to invite them out somewhere away from the office, for example, going out for a cup of coffee. As the two of you relax together, you'll get to hear the real story. Off the record, of course.

G o o d *to* **k n o w** ·······································

● おもてむきは ［omotemuki wa］
● じつは ［jitsu wa］
● ほんねをきく ［honne o kiku］
● しょうじきにいう ［shōjiki ni iu］
● うらのいみ ［ura no imi］
● おちゃでものみませんか。
　［Ocha demo nomimasen ka?］
● ないしょのはなしですが…
　［Naisho no hanashi desu ga ...］

▷ officially
▷ in fact
▷ ask a person's real feelings
▷ to be frank
▷ the hidden meaning or implication
▷ How about going out for a cup of tea or coffee?

▷ This is just between the two of us, but ...

Shame

What's the big deal?

Paula Simpson was impressed with the work done by a subcontractor and told the person in charge she'd like the company to do work on another new project as well. When Paula reported her decision back to her Japanese boss, Ryoji Ono, he looked displeased. Paula asked whether there had been a problem with the subcontractor that she didn't know about, but apparently the general consensus was that the subcontractor had done good work. So why was Ono-*san* looking put out?

Following the proper channels

The problem is not whether the subcontractor is good or bad, but that Paula did not consult her boss first. By not doing so, she has shamed him. **The idea of shame is closely related to face, in Japanese, *mentsu* or *kao*.** Face is a person's public identity. It is socially constructed and relies on each and every person following the proper channels.

The chain of command is strictly hierarchical in Japan. Even before trivial decisions are made, approval from the boss must be sought. Paula's boss expects as a matter of course that he has the right to decide which subcontractor to use. It seems like a personal slight to

him that Paula went ahead without consulting him, even though he would have given approval anyway.

Whether she meant to or not, Paula has made her boss lose face in the department and potentially elsewhere if the story gets out, and that injury is real.

There is not much Paula can do about what's already happened, but she should be very careful to adhere to official procedure from now on. **These are not mere formalities; they are the foundations by which each person's public identity is created.**

Self-generated shame

The other time Japanese people are likely to feel shame is when they are

caught doing something that violates the Japanese definition of common sense, or *jōshiki*. (In this case shame is close to embarrassment.) A very common example is the shame that Japanese people feel if they are somewhere public and they can't remember how to read or write a difficult Japanese *kanji* character.

In this case the feeling of shame can be reduced if the people surrounding him or her pretend they didn't notice the flubup. People are especially careful to say nothing about the mistakes of outsiders or people of higher rank.

If, for example, you notice that someone has made an English spelling error on a document, make sure that you do not draw their attention to it in front of other people. Just remember that they are likely to feel more embarrassed than a Western person in the same situation might.

What about those young people on the trains?

According to traditional Japanese standards of conduct, some Japanese young people in cities have no shame. This is evinced in their public behavior, particularly on trains, such as putting on makeup or even changing their socks. Despite the scowls directed at them by other commuters, they seem unabashed.

However, part of this ability to throw off shame seems to relate to the idea expressed in the traditional saying, *Tabi no haji wa kakisute*: "When on a trip throw away shame," in other words, anything goes. The idea is that no one knows you when you're away from home so you don't have to feel embarrassed. **It is this sense of anonymity that lets them off the hook.** Were their actions to be witnessed by someone who knows them they would most certainly be mortified.

G o o d *to* k n o w ·······································

- ●めんつ・かおをつぶす [*mentsu/kao o tsubusu*]
- ●かおにどろをぬる [*kao ni doro o nuru*]

- ●ないがしろにする [*naigashiro ni suru*]
- ●はじしらず [*haji-shirazu*]
- ●はじをかく [*haji o kaku*]
- ●はずかしいおもいをさせる
  [*hazukashii omoi o saseru*]
- ●ばれる [*bareru*]
- ●うちわのはじをそとにださない
  [*uchiwa no haji o soto ni dasanai*]

▷ shame a person
▷ shame a person (literally, to cover a person's face in mud)

▷ make light of a person or thing
▷ have no sense of shame
▷ bring shame upon oneself
▷ make a person feel ashamed/embarrassed

▷ be disclosed
▷ do not wash one's dirty linen in public

Inference

Are the Japanese mind readers?

In the beginning, Chris and Linda Traney got along well with their next-door neighbors, the Yamamotos, but after about seven months the Yamamotos did not seem as friendly. Finally they indirectly learned that the trees in their garden had gotten so tall that they were blocking sunlight from entering their neighbors' living room. Chris and Linda wondered why the Yamamotos had suffered in annoyance for so long.

How do the Japanese fathom the unsaid?

In Japan there is a lot of communication going on beyond what is actually spoken. This is possible because traditionally many Japanese people have shared the same values so there was little room for misunderstanding. The Japanese version of the English saying "least said, soonest mended" would probably go, **"nothing said, soonest mended, even if it's not yet broken anyway."**

Because of the tendency to avoid direct expression, Japanese people are generally sensitive to facial expression and other nonverbal hints that may indicate another's feelings. This may be frus-

trating to Westerners who remain clueless.

The kinds of feelings that are usually not expressed outright are negative ones — reluctance, disapproval, vexation. However, expressions of romantic feelings or requests for favors are often far from straightforward as well. **The onus is on you to pick up on what's going on.**

Obviously, the Japanese don't have crystal balls. They are able to figure out the situation through a two-step process. First, they are constantly watchful for signs of a person's unstated feelings. Next, like Chris and Linda, **having perceived the presence of some kind of unspoken message they decode it by**

running through a mental checklist of possible causes. The prevention of sunlight is a no-brainer for the Japanese since it is widely known as a source of friction between neighbors.

Why not just ask?

You can try. Asking directly might work, but it might still be difficult for the person to say point-blank what's on his or her mind. Another possibility is to apologize for something (anything!) In so doing, you'll let the person know you're aware of the cold feelings and you want to do something about them, but at the same time also show that you really can't read the situation.

In such a case, the neighbor may vigorously reject your apology while at the same time slip in the suggestion that there is one small thing that you could in fact do for him/her. Ah-ha! Here's the real problem! Even if they don't go that far, they will probably try to be slightly less indirect about what is bugging them. If all else fails, you can ask another Japanese person to gently probe.

What if you don't agree?

Nothing has been said outright. That's the beauty of the system. Therefore, if you understand the predicament but actually would rather not go along with the hints, you can simply pretend that you don't know anything is wrong. Japanese people do it all the time. Of course, the frosty treatment may intensify but it will probably never erupt into open confrontation.

G o o d *to* k n o w ··

- ●はっきりいわない［*hakkiri iwanai*］
- ●とおまわしにいう［*tōmawashi ni iu*］
- ●きをきかす［*ki o kikasu*］
- ●いしんでんしん［*ishin-denshin*］
- ●なにかごめいわくをかけていますか。 ［*Nanika gomeiwaku o kakete imasu ka?*］
- ●しらんかおをする［*shiran-kao o suru*］
- ●びんかんな［*binkanna*］
- ●にぶい・どんかんな［*nibui/donkanna*］
- ●いちをきいてじゅうをしる ［*ichi o kiite jū o shiru*］

▷ not say something directly
▷ beat around the bush
▷ take a hint
▷ unspoken communication
▷ Am I bothering you in some way?

▷ pretend you haven't noticed anything
▷ sensitive
▷ insensitive
▷ derive ten things from one, in other words, understand many deeper implications and meanings

Ambiguity

What do these mixed messages mean?

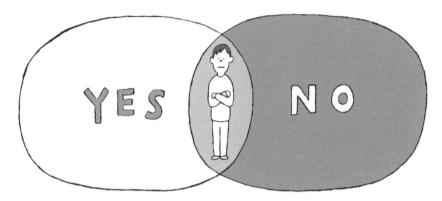

Cheryl Perkins made a presentation to a Japanese company. A company representative told her that they were impressed. Over the next few weeks, Cheryl waited hopefully for more information but received no word. Finally the representative told her that they had decided to go with another company's product. Cheryl couldn't understand why the representative hadn't been clearer to begin with.

When yes means yes

To live in Japan means to develop a tolerance for ambiguity, *aimai*. Are the Japanese always vague? Certainly not. The decision-making process may take longer than in the West, but **if the Japanese are determined about something they will usually make at least some kind of move forward fairly soon**, though generally not right on the spot.

Even if things are stalled for some reason, if they are strongly interested in you they will take the initiative in keeping you in the loop, informing you that the decision may take a little longer, or explaining any hitches that have come up.

On the other hand, keep in mind that you'll virtually always receive polite and encouraging noises during a presentation, interview or whatever. **Being praised means nothing one way or the other.** You may be praised even if they were singularly unimpressed, so try not to take such comments too much to heart. The Japanese are not trying to lead you down the garden path, they are simply being courteous. In general, if there is no follow-up within a couple of weeks, the answer is not yes.

Is absence of a yes a no?

Aimai means the door is not closed. The lack of a positive response following a proposal may mean an absolute no but often it means maybe. There is really no way to tell which it is. The lack of feedback can be frustrating but trying to second-guess is not going to work because pushing will only propel the answer toward no.

Two reasons the Japanese are often reluctant to say no is because they want to protect your feelings and on top of this, a definite negative response is considered rather coarse. But more importantly, **a flatly stated no is generally more irrevocable than in the West.**

This means that the company also cannot change its mind later. The door is not only closed but barred as well. Being in the gray zone with the door slightly ajar is usually preferable for both sides.

Waiting for a yes

The Japanese don't usually like being pressed for a definite yes or no, but they are often impressed by earnestness. If you're not willing to wait for a possible project down the road, move on. You may still be contacted eventually. However, **if you're still interested, it's a good idea to stay in touch in a friendly way.**

The most common ways to do this are through sending seasonal greeting cards as well as any promotional materials or news of you or your company's achievements. The goal is building a relationship with the company, which most companies welcome — it's in their best interest to keep doors open, too.

It is quite possible in Japan to get a phone call a few years later, either from the company you approached or from another company that it has recommended you to. **Let *aimai* work for you.** The Japanese *can* say no, but do you really want them to?

G o o d *to* k n o w ·······························

- ●あいまいなへんじをする [*aimaina henji o suru*]　▷ make a vague answer
- ●あいまいなたいどをとる [*aimaina taido o toru*]　▷ take a vague position
- ●いいかげんなへんじ [*iikagenna henji*]　▷ an evasive answer
- ●ばくぜんと [*bakuzento*]　▷ obscurely
- ●どちらでもない [*dochira demo nai*]　▷ neither yes nor no
- ●もやもやした [*moyamoya-shita*]　▷ hazy, foggy
- ●あやふやな [*ayafuyana*]　▷ equivocal
- ●ふめいな [*fumeina*]　▷ unclear

Diligence

Don't the Japanese like to have fun?

Bob Adams has been working for an importer of health products for six months. He gradually realized that he always seemed to be the first to leave at the end of the day. He also noticed that no one expressed the sentiment "Thank God it's Friday." His colleagues never mentioned that they enjoyed working on a project, either. The successful completion of their work seemed to be their ultimate goal. Were they all workaholics?

Is there life outside the office?

Diligence is respected throughout the world. However, the expression of diligence can differ. Generally speaking, in the West diligence is linked to individuality and pulling yourself up by your own bootstraps. But **the Japanese also associate diligence with the success of the group.**

Because the Japanese sometimes sacrifice their private lives for the sake of their work they can seem like workaholics. But many Japanese get great satisfaction and a feeling of achievement from this group effort, which was a major force propelling Japan's economic success after the World War II.

In addition, **the division between work and private life is more clear-cut than in the West.** It is possible to work side by side with someone for years and never meet his or her spouse or even see a picture. Spouses do not usually drop by the office nor are they invited to company-related social events, such as office parties.

At the same time, many Japanese identify strongly with their company. This is loosening somewhat as lifetime employment decreases. Nonetheless, **most people, when asked what they do, are more likely to say the name of the company they work for than to mention the type of work they themselves are engaged in.**

Rejecting traditional work values

Group-based diligence is weakening in Japan, as witnessed by the *freeters*, so called because they are "free," moving around between various part-time jobs. A distinction is made between this new breed and free-lancers, who may not belong to any one company but show a similar dedication to their work.

Freeters often assert that they'll find meaning in their life outside of work. These young people choose not to seek full-time employment. They prefer instead to work part-time at a variety of jobs just to earn enough money to pursue their other interests, much to the shock and consternation of older generations.

Diligence dos and don'ts

It's perfectly all right to be diligent in your own way. Japanese people don't think badly of a non-Japanese employee leaving earlier than the others if he or she is keeping up with their assigned work.

However, it is a good idea to be careful about two things. First, many people will probably not appreciate being told to "Take it easy" when they are working hard. **Cases may differ, but in general it is better to affirm their diligence by saying *Gambatte!* (You can do it!)** instead. Secondly, never assume that people are not cutting out early on a Friday afternoon like you because they have nothing in their lives besides work.

You may only see one hat in the workplace, but the Japanese wear many hats and one of them is certainly a party hat.

G o o d *to* **k n o w** ·

- ●まじめ [*majime*]　　　　　▷ serious, hardworking
- ●せきにんかん [*sekininkan*]　▷ a sense of responsibility
- ●かいしゃにんげん [*kaisha-ningen*]　▷ someone who lives for the company (disparaging nuance)
- ●くろう [*kurō*]　　　　　　▷ hard work
- ●たいへん [*taihen*]　　　　▷ tough, difficult to accomplish
- ●いそがしい [*isogashii*]　　▷ busy
- ●がんばる [*gambaru*]　　　▷ persevere
- ●どりょく [*doryoku*]　　　▷ effort

Perseverance

Do they never give up?

Fred Daniels has a colleague named Kentaro Saito. Saito-*san* is not happy with the department he has been assigned to because his work interests lay elsewhere. However, he doesn't speak to the general manager about it, nor is he thinking of quitting. When Fred asks him what he's going to do, he says that no matter what he'll stick with the work for three years. Fred wonders why three years. Why not do something about it now if he's not happy?

Three-year stoicism

It is common in the West to move from job to job. In fact, that is often the only way of moving up. But the Japanese put more value on staying in the same place. Many interpret the proverb "A rolling stone gathers no moss" as a caution against too much movement. After all, Japanese people think moss is nice.

The corresponding proverb in Japanese is *Ishi no ue nimo sannen*: "If you sit for three years on a stone you will eventually get warm." It is used to suggest that perseverance brings success. **The idea is to wait and see what you can learn when you're in a tough situation.** That is *gaman*. Endurance without complaint is an aesthetic value. On the

other hand, speaking out soon is seen as selfish.

Putting in the time

To be thought of as *akippoi*, frivolous or flighty, is something most Japanese will try to avoid at all costs. Once you have set your mind to do something and have publicly expressed your intention, by joining a company or even something as inconsequential as taking up a new hobby, you stick with it, no matter what.

There is a perception that it is childish to quit until you've given it a thorough trial. In explaining why they are continuing something which they themselves admit is not working out, Japanese people often say, *Kimeta koto desu kara*:

"Because it's something I decided to do."

In most cases, you have to pay your dues. If a person starts work in one company and gets a better offer from another company the following year, he or she can move on and many do. But the move is made at a cost. People see the person as someone who doesn't have enough perseverance. **Personnel officers often look suspiciously at those who have changed jobs frequently and ask why.**

It can't be helped?

Gaman is a positive value. However, *gaman* can sometimes turn into a passive resignation as expressed in the phrase *Shikata ga nai*, which means, "It can't be helped." Obviously, there is a time to toe the line and a time to draw the line. The emphasis put on hanging in there occasionally has tragic consequences —

employees die of overwork and high school athletes collapse during rigorous training.

Recently, the idea of *gaman* has been changing, with more emphasis on each person knowing his or her own pace and limit. You don't need to wait three years, but it might be a good idea to try counting to ten.

G o o d *to* **k n o w** ·

- ●がまんづよい [*gaman-zuyoi*]　▷ stoical
- ●がまんする [*gaman-suru*]　▷ endure
- ●にんたい [*nintai*]　▷ patience, fortitude
- ●がまんできない [*gaman dekinai*]　▷ unbearable, unendurable
- ●しかたがない。[*Shikata ga nai.*]　▷ It can't be helped.
- ●あきらめる [*akirameru*]　▷ give up
- ●もんく [*monku*]　▷ a complaint
- ●もんくをいわない [*monku o iwanai*]　▷ uncomplaining
- ●なきごと [*nakigoto*]　▷ whining

Consideration for Others

Busybody or busy helping?

Pricilla Matthews is expecting a baby in four months. Her Japanese friends give her rather too much advice. Her husband, who is Japanese, says that this is *omoiyari*, consideration for others. But Pricilla feels like screaming out "Excuse me, but I can take care of myself!"

Looking out for others

Omoiyari means to put the needs of others ahead of your own and this is a very important value in Japan. From childhood, Japanese people are told that those who are considerate to others will be respected. On the other hand, self-centeredness is seen as something very negative.

This pattern of behavior plays a vital role in Japanese communication. **Because Japanese people are reluctant to ask for help, especially regarding private matters, those around them feel they must take the lead in acting on their assumptions and offering advice.**

Of course, they could, and sometimes do, simply say, "If you need anything, just let me know." But taking a more active approach is a way of showing a sincere willingness to help. This can make it easier for the other person to ask for help when they need it.

Too much of a good thing?

Most Japanese don't know that Westerners are comfortable asking for help when they need it and that unsought advice can feel like an invasion of privacy. They worry that someone living in a foreign country must be confused and frustrated so they take it upon themselves to help out of kindness.

No doubt, Pricilla's friends are concerned that Pricilla may be anxious about giving birth away from home and are trying their best to make her feel at ease. They have no idea that their kindness is having the opposite effect.

Sometimes Japanese people's expression of concern can seem exceedingly commanding. When giving advice they often use expressions such as "... *shite wa dame!*" (You definitely shouldn't ...) or "... *shinai to mazui yo!*" (It would be a really bad idea to not...) **The insistent, imperative tone is seen as a way of showing care, rather than as a means of compelling you to accept their recommendation.**

Thanks but no thanks

This does not mean you have to accept all the guidance or assistance being offered left and right. However, **if you want to get along with the Japanese it is better to avoid an explicit rejection of *omoiyari* even if you sometimes feel irritated.**

While the advice is given vigorously, Japanese people are very quick to take the hint if you're not interested. Japanese people hate meddling, *osekkai*, which is prompted not by consideration for the other person but by a person's own curiosity. At times they may seem the same but consideration and meddling are very different.

When receiving advice, you can just smile and do nothing. You can also say gently, *Daijōbu desu* (I'm fine.) The goal for the Japanese showing consideration is not to get you to do what they want, but to help you do what you want. In all cases, remember to think of the position of the person who is thinking of your position.

G o o d *to* **k n o w** ··

● きがきく ［*ki ga kiku*］ ▷ be considerate
● しんぱいをかけてすみません。 ▷ Thank you for worrying about me.
  ［*Shimpai o kakete sumimasen.*］
● きくばりをする ［*kikubari o suru*］ ▷ care about others
● おせわになる ［*osewa ni naru*］ ▷ be taken care of
● めんどうをみる ［*mendō o miru*］ ▷ take care of (a person)
● おもいやりがない ［*omoiyari ga nai*］ ▷ thoughtless
● よけいなおせわ ［*yokeina osewa*］ ▷ meddling in a person's affairs
● たちいる ［*tachiiru*］ ▷ interfere
● かどがたつ ［*kado ga tatsu*］ ▷ offend

Bullying

What did I do wrong?

Chris Turner works in the sales department of a manufacturer of VCRs. When he sold more units than anyone else in his department for three consecutive months, Chris's boss seemed delighted but his colleagues became increasingly cold. A few began to deliberately hinder his work, not passing on telephone messages or not informing him of meetings. Were these people adults or what?

Blaming the victim

Chris's situation is a case of office *ijime*. **Ijime is usually translated as bullying but it basically means giving somebody a hard time.** While it is mainly done by a few people, the whole group is usually complicit. In recent years *ijime* has become a major social problem in Japan, particularly among schoolchildren. These children are often the victims of repeated physical assaults and in the worst cases suicide is the tragic result.

There is a saying in Japanese, *Deru kugi wa utareru*: "The nail that sticks out gets hammered down." Those who are harassed are usually somewhat different from the rest, which the others perceive as willful and conceited. **It is not uncommon to hear the opinion that the victim is at fault.** The attitude is that if only that person would try to get along with the rest, there would be no problem. Many victims simply endure the *ijime*, which seems to fuel increasing levels of it.

But I didn't do anything!

Any difference is a potential cause of *ijime*. A typical criticism of those who are targets is *erasōni*, which means to be haughty or put on airs. This reproach is usually quite unfair: most people take pains to not appear proud. However, **not appearing proud is not enough, the difference itself must be reduced.**

For example, foreign businesswomen often complain of harassment by female colleagues. The conflict usually stems from a situation in which the Japanese women feel they must perform some traditionally female duties such as serving tea and collecting the teacups after a meeting. They resent the foreign woman who feels no compunction in turning a blind eye to these duties.

Japanese people know that foreigners are different but they often feel that foreigners should try to lessen the distinction whenever possible. From the Japanese women's point of view, it's just a few teacups. They feel that showing solidarity is more important than making it plain that you're above such menial tasks. The bottom line is **if you really can't go along with something, don't, but try to adapt where you can.**

Pulling others up

If you have special skills, you should use them. Obviously, Chris shouldn't try to sell fewer units in order not to stand out. But if he wants to get along better with his colleagues he should try to use his talents to pull the others up with him.

In elementary schools children belong to small groups, called *han*. Teachers are more likely to praise the good student who helped a poorer student than one who spent more time expanding his or her own skills. This pattern of thinking is replicated in the working world. **By all means try to achieve personal glory, but at the same time keep your eye on the glory of the whole group.** By doing so you'll be the victor, not the victim.

G o o d *to* k n o w ·

- ●しごとをじゃまする [*shigoto o jama-suru*] ▷ interfere with (another's) work
- ●いばる [*ibaru*] ▷ be arrogant
- ●ごうまんなたいどをとる [*gōmanna taido o toru*] ▷ assume a proud attitude
- ●いばしょがない [*ibasho ga nai*] ▷ without a place (due to ostracism)
- ●むしする [*mushi-suru*] ▷ ostracize
- ●なかまはずれになる [*nakama-hazure ni naru*] ▷ be shunned
- ●むらはちぶ [*mura-hachibu*] ▷ social ostracism
- ●わがまま [*wagamama*] ▷ egotistical
- ●こりつする [*koritsu-suru*] ▷ become isolated

Moral Obligation

Who is a trustworthy person?

Tracey William's colleague, Naoya Otsuka, is incredibly busy at work. In spite of this, when he received an invitation from a senior member of his university tennis circle to go out, Otsuka-*san* immediately accepted. Otsuka-*san* told Tracey he had *giri* (obligation) toward senior members of the club. Tracey had heard this word before but she still didn't really understand it.

Affirming reciprocal bonds

Giri is a kind of moral obligation. **If someone has helped a person in the past, that person will continue to demonstrate his or her gratitude by supporting the other in any way possible.** Showing up at a party may seem like a small thing, but by doing so Otsuka-*san* is making it clear that the senior member can rely on him.

Many Japanese people go to great lengths to attend these kinds of gatherings. They feel it will make the person to whom they owe a debt of gratitude look bad if they don't. Also, **it is through these small gestures that the reciprocal bond is affirmed.** *Giri* is like a ball tossed back and forth between two peo-

ple. The game of catch creates a "we're-in-this-together" feeling that Japanese people thrive on.

In kabuki and literature, *giri* is often contrasted with *ninjō*, kindheartedness, with themes in which the main character is forced to make a choice between love and duty. In everyday life, however, *giri* and *ninjō* often are seen as two sides of the same coin.

Obligation in the workplace

It is essential to understand the role of *giri* when doing business in Japan. Often two companies have a relationship of give and take based on a sense of moral obligation. **In deciding which company to work with on a given project, these** ties of obligation are one factor in the decision-making process. It is possible for a weaker company to be chosen to execute a project because of such considerations.

The other time you'll hear the word *giri* a lot in offices is on Valentine's Day. In Japan, women give men chocolate rather than vice-versa. Even if they don't particularly like them, female employees give chocolate to all their male counterparts. This is called *giri choko* (obligation chocolate).

It's another recognition of mutual support. The men in turn give a small present of white chocolate or some cookies on the so-called "White Day" a month later to show that they also acknowledge the ties.

Building trust

One of the best things that can be said about a person is that they have a strong sense of obligation. This means that they can be relied upon when the chips are down. In turn, others are willing to help this kind of person even if they themselves have not as yet been the direct beneficiary of that person's good deeds.

Try to help colleagues when you can, even if your assistance is not directly related to the work at hand. In return, when someone helps you, make sure that you remember what he or she has done for you. In addition to thanking the person at the time, try to find ways to repay their kindness. **The more favors you grant and receive, the more you'll be trusted.**

Understanding *giri* and building relationships based on it will strengthen your position in your company and make it easier for you to accomplish your work.

Good to know

●ぎりがある [*giri ga aru*]	▷ have an obligation
●ぎりがたい [*girigatai*]	▷ possess a strong sense of obligation
●ぎりをはたす [*giri o hatasu*]	▷ perform one's duty
●ふぎり [*fugiri*]	▷ ingratitude
●おぎりに [*ogiri-ni*]	▷ perfunctorily
●ぎりをかく [*giri o kaku*]	▷ neglect one's duties
●ぎりとにんじょうのいたばさみとなる [*giri to ninjō no itabasami to naru*]	▷ be torn between love and duty
●おんにむくいる [*on ni mukuiru*]	▷ repay a debt of gratitude

Modesty

Why sell yourself short?

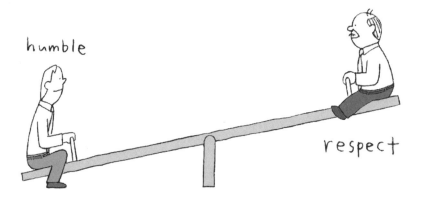

humble

respect

Marion Smith was invited to the home of her colleague, Tatsuya Makiura. When she arrived, Makiura-*san* said, "My house is very small and dirty but please come in." But when Marion was shown into the living room she was surprised to see that the house was very spacious, elegant, and spotlessly clean. Why did Makiura-*san* make such an obviously untrue comment?

On a seesaw

Makiura-*san* was showing modesty, or *kenson*, by speaking in this way. **Showing modesty is a means of expressing respect.** Picture a seesaw. The prevailing notion here is that if I go down, you go up. At times, the seesaw can really take off as both parties try to outdo each other in putting themselves down in order to elevate the other.

This system is embedded in the Japanese language itself. There is a humble form of speech, called *kenjō*, which people use to refer to themselves, their families and their companies. Basic verbs such as *be*, *have*, *do* and *go* have separate words that include a tone of humility, signifying "humbly be,"

"humbly have," "humbly do" and "humbly go."

In addition, people refer to their own company as *heisha*, literally "a bad company." Learning to use this kind of language smoothly and appropriately is a part of company training for new employees fresh to the world of business.

Don't believe it

If you're not used to the system it can seem as if the person is either fishing for compliments or has a severe inferiority complex. However, **the self-deprecation does not have any literal meaning.** It is important to not take the words at face value. To do so would hurt the other person's feelings.

Someone who has been practicing tea ceremony might say they are a mere novice and can't do anything right, yet you could find out later that they have been practicing regularly for 20 years!

When someone says something belittling their own skills or possessions you should never agree or act as if you believe them. On the other hand, even if you know they don't really mean what they're saying, it is important to explicitly reject the surface meaning of their comments. If you don't know the person well, you can say, "I'm sure that's not true" or if you do know them, then you can emphatically deny the assertion saying, "That's certainly not true!"

Happily married

Showing modesty about one's family is an area where there are often cross-cultural misunderstandings. It's one thing to disparage yourself, but **Westerners are sometimes puzzled or even offended by Japanese men who put down their wives**, saying that they aren't beautiful, can't cook well, or are *gusai*, foolish wives.

Women, for their part, sometimes speak of their husbands as though they were incompetents hanging about and getting in the way at home. This doesn't mean the husbands or wives really think this.

A Japanese person would feel very uncomfortable praising their family. However, **most Japanese people think it's great when Western men say how wonderful their wives are and vice-versa.** In the end, it doesn't matter whether you say "my great husband" or "my lazy husband," it's the actual relationship that counts.

G o o d *to* **k n o w** ···

- ●ひかえめ［*hikaeme*］
- ●つつしみ［*tsutsushimi*］
- ●こんなわたし［*konna watashi*］
- ●ぜんぜんできません。［*Zenzen dekimasen.*］
- ●…がへたです。［*... ga heta desu.*］
- ●たいしたことはできませんが…
  ［*Taishita koto wa dekimasen ga ...*］
- ●そんなことないでしょう。
  ［*Sonna koto nai deshō.*］
- ●そんなことないですよ。
  ［*Sonna koto nai desu yo.*］

- ▷ with reserve
- ▷ modesty
- ▷ a person like me (used when speaking modestly)
- ▷ I can't do it at all.
- ▷ I'm not good at ...
- ▷ I can't do much but ...
  (used when making an offer to help)
- ▷ I'm sure that's not true.
- ▷ That's certainly not true.

Face to Face with the Japanese

Meeting Someone for the First Time

Starting off on the right foot

bowing

When Phil Edwards was introduced to a client, Makoto Bamba, he stuck out his hand at the same time that Bamba-*san* bowed. Then Bamba-*san* presented his business card to Phil very gracefully as Phil was still scrabbling around trying to get his own business card out of his pocket. He worried that he wasn't giving a very good first impression.

Not in a hurry

Shaking hands is not a Japanese custom. **When meeting a foreign person, some Japanese people will stick out their hand, while most others will bow.** It is a good idea to pay attention to what the other person is doing. If the other person starts to extend their hand, then shake it. If they start to bow, it's better to bow as well. As long as you don't automatically assume that you will be shaking hands you can probably avoid what happened to Phil.

Don't be concerned if little eye contact takes place: there is less of a cultural emphasis on looking people squarely in the eye in Japan. It doesn't mean the other person is unenthusiastic about working with you or untrustworthy. Without a firm handshake or eye contact your best bet for gaining a first impression is in the bow.

Ins and outs of bowing

The Japanese know that bowing, or *ojigi*, is not a Western custom so you don't need to worry about this if you don't want to. But bowing can be very useful as a means of expressing hello and goodbye without ever opening your mouth. As you live in Japan you might find yourself beginning to bow naturally.

There are basically two types of bows. With friends, you simply incline your body slightly. This kind of bow is called an *eshaku*. In a normal business situation you bow more deeply, about 45 degrees, keeping your back straight and pausing for one beat before rising. **Men keep their hands at their sides and women cross their hands below their stomachs.**

You can surreptitiously watch what the people around you are doing to figure out when to straighten up. **Try to avoid straightening up too soon — foreigners have a tendency to bob up and down several times which the Japanese find highly amusing.**

Graceful business card exchanges

After shaking hands or bowing, you will exchange business cards, or *meishi*. This is a big deal. **The Japanese take the exchanging of business cards seriously.** All the important information for a successful first meeting is on the card, including the person's department and rank in the company.

There is no need to scrabble around. You can and should take the time to do it properly. **The goal is to make a little ceremony of the business card exchange,** not to get through it as quickly as possible.

Remove your card carefully and extend it with both hands toward the other person so that the printed information is facing him or her. You will accept his or her card in the same way.

When you take the card it is considered polite to study it for a moment and make some small talk, for example, commenting on the person's name or the location of the company.

You'll do fine as long as you approach the bow or handshake and the exchange of business cards with a little more formality than you might in the West. If you stick to this basic point, no matter what happens, the other person is sure to feel that it truly was nice to meet you.

G o o d *to* **k n o w** ···

● はじめまして。[*Hajimemashite.*]

▷ It's nice to meet you. (used only on first meetings)

● …ともうします。[*... to mōshimasu.*]

▷ My name is ...

● よろしくおねがいします。
  [*Yoroshiku onegai-shimasu.*]

▷ I look forward to working with you/getting to know you. (This can be used when you first meet the person and/or as you say goodbye.)

● これはみょうじですか。
  [*Kore wa myōji desu ka?*]

▷ Is this your last/family name?

● わたしを…とよんでください。
  [*Watashi o ... to yonde kudasai.*]

▷ Please call me ...

● おじぎ [*ojigi*]

▷ bowing

● めいし [*meishi*]

▷ a business card

Hellos and Goodbyes

Doesn't *sayonara* mean goodbye?

I+tekimasu.

I+terasshai.

Vanessa Lamb didn't know a lot of Japanese but one word she thought she didn't have to worry about was *sayonara*. However, as she used it in everyday encounters, Vanessa noticed that she seemed to be using it more often than the Japanese people around her, who were using a variety of other expressions. Vanessa wanted to know other ways of saying goodbye so she could sound more natural.

Everyday verbal interactions

In the countryside, people may greet everyone who passes by. However, in the city it is more likely that people will only speak to people they know.

There is a definite social script for the words spoken in business and personal situations with colleagues, clients, family members and neighbors. **Because these expressions are so widely applicable it's definitely worth it to take the time to learn them.**

As you look at the phrases introduced here you will notice that **rather than a generic "hello," Japanese greetings change depending on the time of day or situation.**

Also, *sayonara* has not been included. *Sayonara* does mean goodbye but it can have a pretty heavy meaning. It is used when you won't see the person for a long while or perhaps never again. For example, lovers say it when they break up. **In general, non-native speakers of Japanese overuse *sayonara*.**

Of course, Japanese people understand the English words "hello" and "goodbye," but if you learn the following Japanese phrases, you'll be rewarded with happy smiles on the faces of your acquaintances.

Hellos

Time of day / Situation	Japanese phrase	English meaning
❶ In the morning	*Ohayō (gozaimasu).* おはよう（ございます）。	Good morning.
❷ In the afternoon	*Konnichiwa.* こんにちは。	Good afternoon.
❸ In the evening	*Kombanwa.* こんばんは。	Good evening.
❹ When returning to your house, neighborhood, or office the same day or when returning from a trip	Person returning: *Tadaima.* ただいま。 Person already there: *Okaerinasai.* おかえりなさい。	I'm home. Welcome back.

Goodbyes

❶ When leaving a house, neighborhood, or office with the intention of returning that day or when leaving on a trip	Person leaving: *Ittekimasu.* いってきます。 Person remaining behind: *Itterasshai.* いってらっしゃい。	I'm leaving./I'll be back. See you later.
❷ When leaving the office at the end of the day	Person leaving: *Osaki ni (shitsurei-shimasu).* おさきに（しつれいします）。 Person remaining: *Otsukaresama (deshita).* おつかれさま（でした）。	Well, I'm done for the day. (literally, "I'm going first.") OK. Bye. (literally, "You must be tired from the work.")
❸ When saying goodbye at business meetings	Person leaving: *Kore de shitsurei-shimasu.* これでしつれいします。 Person remaining: *Arigatō gozaimashita.* ありがとうございました。 Either person: *Yoroshiku onegai-shimasu.* よろしくおねがいします。	I'll take my leave now. Thank you very much. I look forward to our continuing work together.

What to Call People

What did you say your name was?

**Nancy Evans met a client who said to her in English, "My name is Hori."
Therefore Nancy called him Hori throughout the meeting. It was only later
that she found out that Hori was the man's last name, not his first name. She
wondered what she should have called him.**

Infrequent firsts

Japanese names, when spoken in
Japanese, begin with the family name
followed by the given name (first name).
This means that **in Japanese the "first
name" is the family name and the "last
name" is the given name.** When ascer-
taining a person's name it's safer to stick
with the words family name and given
name, which cause less confusion.

If you are only told one name, like "My
name is Hori," which is often the case,
you can be pretty sure that it is the family
name. It is rare to call another person by
their first name in Japan. **Generally you
will call a person by their family name,
with -san, which means Mr. or Ms., at
the end.**

Occasionally, female colleagues who
are close may call each other by their
first names. But particularly when talking to a colleague of the opposite sex, it
is a wise idea to stick with the last name
(family name). If not, you may be suggesting a greater degree of intimacy than
you intend.

Hey you!

There are various words that mean
"you" in Japanese: the most common are
anata, used by both men and women,
and *kimi* and *omae* used primarily by
men. However, **words meaning "you"
are usually used in very casual circumstances and even then not always.**
The Japanese language does not require a

grammatical subject and when it is obvious who you are speaking to you do not need to use "you" or any other name. However, when it is necessary to specify, you can call the person directly by his or her name or title.

If you are speaking to the person in their capacity as the holder of a particular position it is customary to refer to them by that title. This can be very convenient when you have forgotten someone's name.

Same group?

In addition, **the ways you use to refer to people depend on whether you are speaking to someone in the same group as you, for example, people in your family or company, or to someone outside your group.** When speaking to an outsider the Japanese use humble words to refer to themselves, their family members and co-workers. For example, if you are referring to a colleague when speaking to a client you will not attach -*san* to their last name.

There are various words to refer to one's wife, the most popular being *kanai* or *tsuma,* while the word used to refer to another person's wife is *okusan.* Words for a woman's own husband include *shujin, danna* and *otto.* The first two mean "master" so **many women currently prefer the less sexist *otto.*** However, it's hard to get way from a touch of feudalism when referring to another woman's husband since the main choices, *goshujin* and *danna-san,* also mean "master."

G o o d *to* k n o w ·······································

● みょうじ [*myōji*]　　　▷ a last/family name
● したのなまえ　　　　　▷ given name (literally, the "name underneath" since when written
　[*shita no namae*]　　　　vertically the given name would be under the family name)

◆**What to call family members**

There are two forms: the humble form is used when talking about your own family. The respectful form is used when talking about another person's family members. In the examples below the humble form is on the left and the respectful form is on the right.

● father: ちち [*chichi*] — おとうさん [*otōsan*]

● mother: はは [*haha*] — おかあさん [*okāsan*]

● elder brother: あに [*ani*] — おにいさん [*onīsan*]

● elder sister: あね [*ane*] — おねえさん [*onēsan*]

● younger brother: おとうと [*otōto*] — おとうとさん [*otōto-san*]

● younger sister: いもうと [*imōto*] — いもうとさん [*imōto-san*]

● son: むすこ [*musuko*] — むすこさん [*musuko-san*] (or ごしそく [*goshisoku*])

● daughter: むすめ [*musume*] — むすめさん [*musume-san*] (or おじょうさん [*ojō-san*])

(When talking directly to one's own father, mother, elder brother or sister, the respectful form is also used.)

Nonverbal Communication

What does that gesture mean?

Kathy Mahoney discussed with her boss, Hajime Shimada, an idea she had for a new business venture. As she spoke, Shimada-*san* kept nodding so Kathy felt quite encouraged. But at the end of her pitch, Shimada-*san* said that he didn't think the venture was possible. If he didn't like the idea why had he kept on nodding?

What is that person doing?

Gestures are by no means universal. What Kathy didn't realize is that in Japan, nodding only means that you are listening, not that you agree. The illustrations and explanations below show some of the Japanese gestures that are often difficult for Westerners to interpret. Understanding them will save you a lot of confusion.

Folding your arms in front of your chest is used by men to indicate skepticism, reluctance or bewilderment. It can look fairly confrontational but is considered softer than voicing these opinions or feelings outright. It can also simply mean that the man doing it is trying to think of what to say or has nothing to do at the moment.

Scratching the back of your head indicates embarrassment because a mistake has been made or some secret has been revealed. It can also indicate the person is thinking of the answer to a difficult question. It is used mostly by men.

Raising your hands over your head and touching them to form a circle means "OK." Conversely, making a large "X" with your hands in front of you means "No good." Basically, they are equivalents of thumbs up or thumbs down.

Waving your hand from side to side shows modesty after or during being complimented or praised. It can also be used to express "You shouldn't have!" when someone gives you a present.

Pressing your two hands together is used when making a request or thanking someone for performing a favor. It is also used when apologizing for small matters such as being late to meet someone at a train station.

An up-and-down motion with the right hand is used to ask someone to make room for you, either when you are trying to walk through a crowd or if you're trying to sit down between two people on a train. This gesture is mostly used by men.

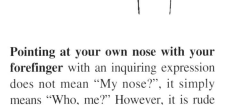

Pointing at your own nose with your forefinger with an inquiring expression does not mean "My nose?", it simply means "Who, me?" However, it is rude to point at other people's noses.

Beckoning with your palm down means "Come here." Suggestive as it is of a limp wrist, it can look very strange at first, but it is the usual method of summoning someone and you will probably not see Japanese people motion to you with their palms up.

Expressing Gratitude

How do you say thank you?

Pete Davis gave a close colleague, Yukitoshi Suzuki, a book of photographs of his hometown, Boston. Pete and Suzuki-*san* had often discussed Boston because Suzuki-*san* had also spent some time there as a student. Pete thought Suzuki-*san* would enjoy the book, but when he gave it to him, Suzuki-*san* said, *Sumimasen.* Pete knew *sumimasen* meant "sorry" and wondered why Suzuki-*san* was apologizing.

Fluidity of function

Flip through an English-Japanese dictionary and it will tell you that "thank you" in Japanese is *arigatō*. **Arigatō is used often but just as often you'll hear *sumimasen*. *Sumimasen* is used both as an expression of gratitude and as an apology.** Other words of apology, such as the more formal *mōshiwake nai*, can also be used in thanking people.

Because of this fluidity of function, **Japanese people see less of a distinction between apologies and thanks.** In essence, to thank someone is to apologize for the trouble that they have gone to on your behalf.

Who do you thank?

The answer to this question seems easy. You thank anyone who has helped you in some way or given you something, right? Yes, but this begs the question of how help is defined.

The Japanese do not usually say thank you in some situations in which Western people typically do. For example, **family members rarely thank each other.** They are not unappreciative of each other, but the idea that each will help the other is taken for granted. To say thank you would suggest a less intimate relationship.

Another obvious case is service encounters. **If a Japanese person buys something at a store or exchanges** money at the bank they will probably **not say thank you,** even though the clerk will. This does not seem cold or haughty to the Japanese. They see no reason to express gratitude because the other person has simply done their job. On the other hand, if someone did something above and beyond the call of their duties, they would be sure to be thanked.

Multiple thank-yous

Thanking is often a two- or three- step process. **Japanese people thank a person when he or she does something for them. Then they thank him or her again right before parting ways and/or the next time they meet.**

In business, if you are treated to lunch or dinner, it is common etiquette to call the next day to say thank you again. After a meal at a person's home, many Japanese send a thank-you note.

It's often easier to remember the feeling of gratitude than to remember the specifics. This is true for the Japanese as well and so **there is a blanket thank-you that can be used when you thank someone again for something they did several days before:** *Senjitsu wa arigatō gozaimashita*, simply "Thank you for the other day."

When you first come to Japan you will probably get a lot of help from various people. At times like this, knowing this phrase can really help.

G o o d *to* **k n o w** ·····································

● どうも。[*Dōmo.*]
　▷ Thanks. (a casual way of expressing gratitude)
● どうもありがとう。[*Dōmo arigatō.*]
　▷ Thank you very much. (*Dōmo* in this case means "very much.")
● おそれいります。[*Osore-irimasu.*]
　▷ It's very kind of you. (This includes the characters meaning "to have fear" and can also be used to apologize.)
● きょうしゅくです。[*Kyōshuku desu.*]
　▷ I'm obliged to you. (This includes the characters meaning "to shrink with fear" and is also used when making requests.)
● いつもありがとうございます。
　[*Itsumo arigatō gozaimasu.*]
　▷ Thank you for your help all the time.
● たすかりました。[*Tasukarimashita.*]
　▷ You were a big help.
● ごくろうさま。[*Gokurō sama.*]
　▷ Thanks for your trouble. (used to thank a person in a subordinate position)

Apologizing

Are you really and truly sorry?

Anna Sullivan had arranged to meet her accountant, Satoshi Ueda, at a coffee shop midway between their offices. Anna arrived on time and waited but Ueda-*san* never showed up. Anna called her office and learned that Ueda-*san* had left a message that it was impossible for him to keep their appointment. The following day Ueda-*san* visited her office with a box of cookies and repeatedly expressed how sorry he was to have missed the appointment. However, he never gave an explanation for his negligence.

No reason given

Anna's situation with Ueda-*san* is typical. For many Westerners, hearing an account of why something went amiss is an integral part of an apology. It is important for the wrongdoer to assert that the action was unintentional and unavoidable.

In Japan, however, this is a much less vital portion of expressing regret. Japanese people may give an explanation for a small slip-up. But **in cases where another person is seriously inconvenienced, explanations are seen as excuses, a way of diminishing one's responsibility for the trouble, and sometimes even superfluous to the matter at hand.**

Ueda-*san* probably has a good reason for having missed the appointment but feels that that good reason, especially if unrelated to anything to do with Anna, does not make up for the trouble he has caused her.

From his point of view, it's more appropriate not to mention it at all but rather try to set things right by taking the trouble to go to her office and express his heartfelt regret.

Levels of regret

There are various words to express regret. A lot depends on how sorry the person who did something wrong feels. Also, the tone of voice and body language, such as how deeply the person bows, have a big impact on how the apology is perceived. But basically, **casual words of apology include *shitsurei*, *sumimasen* and *gomen*.**

Shitsurei is an acknowledgement that a social rule has been violated, similar to "Excuse me." This word is often used if you bump into someone, for example. *Sumimasen* and *gomen* can also be used in this kind of situation as well as slighter bigger blunders, like forgetting to return a book.

As the wrongdoing increases in severity, you are more likely to hear *gomennasai, taihen shitsurei-shimashita,* and *mōshiwake arimasen*.

Self-reflection

In addition to an outright statement of regret or an explanation of the events

contributing to a problem, there are two other common ways to apologize. One way is to try to do something to make the situation better and the other is assuring the offended party that the same thing won't happen again. Also, like Ueda-*san*, **businesspeople who have flubbed up somehow often bring a present when they apologize.**

On top of that, they will usually promise to be careful in the future. **One of the most frequently heard words in earnest apologies is *hansei-shite imasu*, which means that you have reflected on your conduct.** If you make a serious blunder in Japan you'll go a long way toward restoring good will if you use this magic phrase.

G o o d *to* k n o w ∙∙∙∙∙∙∙∙∙∙∙∙∙∙∙∙∙∙∙∙∙∙∙∙∙∙∙∙∙∙∙∙∙∙∙∙∙∙

- ●すみません。[*Sumimasen.*]
- ●ごめんなさい。[*Gomennasai.*]
- ●しつれいしました。[*Shitsurei-shimashita.*]
- ●あやまる [*ayamaru*]
- ●しゃざいする [*shazai-suru*]
- ●おわび [*owabi*]
- ●いいわけ [*iiwake*]
- ●いいわけをしない [*iiwake o shinai*]
- ●ゆるす [*yurusu*]
- ●こうかいする [*kōkai-suru*]
- ●わたしがわるかったです。
  [*Watashi ga warukatta desu.*]

- ▷ I'm sorry. (literally, "The matter isn't settled.")
- ▷ Forgive me. (literally, "Please permit me.")
- ▷ Excuse me. (literally, "I lost my manners.")
- ▷ apologize
- ▷ make an official apology
- ▷ an apology
- ▷ an excuse
- ▷ make no excuse
- ▷ forgive
- ▷ regret
- ▷ It's my fault. (literally, "I was bad.")

Complimenting

Why is it a feast or famine?

Jim Clark has been working for a Japanese company for two years. He put a lot of effort in, especially recently while he was preparing for a presentation. The presentation went very well but his boss didn't even say anything about it. On the other hand, it seems wherever else he goes he is complimented all the time. Why is his own company the one place that refuses to acknowledge his good points?

Taken for granted

In general, Japanese companies do not give much feedback to their employees if things are going well. If there is any explicit assessment it is usually negative. This can be hard if you're used to the positive reinforcement of praise. However, it is evidence that you're an insider because **compliments are usually given to outsiders.**

If you're really concerned about how people in the office feel about your work you can always ask for an evaluation. You'll probably be reassured to find out that your boss's silence did not mean there was any problem. On the other hand, he or she probably still won't go overboard in their commendation.

The basic Japanese approach to staff development is drawing attention to areas that need improvement rather than complimenting work well done. Just bear in mind that no news is good news and learn to give yourself your own pat on the back.

Elaborate praise for outsiders

Compliments given to outsiders tend to be lavish. Complimenting is a way of being polite and outsiders are praised as a matter of course without much regard to real assessment. Therefore **it is important to not get too carried away if a person talks at length about what a wonderful and talented person you**

are. Take it to mean "I want a good relationship with you" rather than "I believe you're God's gift to man."

At the same time, Japanese people don't like excessive flattery, *oseji*. This is because they suspect that the person is making fun of them. **There is an expression in Japanese *homegoroshi*, which means to kill someone through excessive praise.** But it's highly unlikely that this is their purpose in complimenting you.

Responding to compliments

Foreign people are frequently told how good their Japanese is even if they only speak a few words of it. On the other hand, if a Japanese person who speaks English well is similarly complimented, they will usually laugh it off or say, "Far from it!" These are typical responses to compliments in Japan because people don't want to seem vain.

When Japanese people agree with a positive assessment and don't feel like brushing it aside, they usually say, "I'm honored to be told this by a person like you" or comment on the effort that they put into the attainment of the skill or quality that is being praised.

The giving and receiving of compliments is a basic social function. As long as you remember the somewhat different ground rules in Japan you'll do fine.

G o o d *to* **k n o w** ··

●ほめる [*homeru*]
▷ compliment

●たかくひょうかする [*takaku hyōka-suru*]
▷ evaluate highly

●もんだいないですね。[*Mondai nai desu ne.*]
▷ There's no problem.

●わるくないですね。[*Waruku nai desu ne.*]
▷ It's all right.

●すてきですね。[*Suteki desu ne.*]
▷ How pretty!

●すばらしいですね。[*Subarashii desu ne.*]
▷ How wonderful!

●とてもゆうのうなひとです。
[*Totemo yūnōna hito desu.*]
▷ (You're) very talented.

●もちあげる [*mochiageru*]
▷ praise a person to the skies

●そんなことないですよ。
[*Sonna koto nai desu yo.*]
▷ Not really.

●まだまだです。[*Madamada desu.*]
▷ I still have a long way to go.

Invitations

What just took place?

Do you like parties?

Why is she asking me this?

Keiko Takahashi, a colleague, approached Claire Andrews in early December and asked if she had ever pounded rice for New Year's. Claire responded affirmatively. Takahashi-*san* looked crestfallen and said "Oh ..." When Claire asked why she had asked, Takahashi-*san* said that she had hoped to invite Claire to her rice-pounding. Claire said "Oh," and smiled but the situation was awkward and no further invitation was extended.

Vague openings

Japanese invitations are a process of negotiation requiring the cooperation of both sides to take place. They often start off very generally, for example, **"Have you ever ...?" or "Do you like parties?"**

Most Japanese people recognize immediately the possibility that an invitation is forthcoming. These neutral questions are used to explore the other person's interest. Invitations may be adapted or simply abandoned depending on the response.

The person doing the inviting doesn't want to impose on the other person. Japanese people rarely say something along the lines of "I'd really like it if you could come" for fear of

applying too much pressure. By framing her question as she did, Takahashi-*san* gave Claire an out. If Claire didn't want to take up her rice-pounding proposal then the situation ended perfectly.

Takahashi-*san* was waiting for a go-ahead signal from Claire that did not come. If Claire wanted to go, she needed to say something like how much she enjoyed going last year and was hoping for a chance to go again.

Non-invitations

Sometimes things that seem to be invitations are not. **A typical way Japanese people move on from one topic to the next is by making some sort of vague statement of future plans** concerning the first topic, such as "Let's ... some-time." Because people often talk about where they live when they first meet, it is common to say, "Please come to my house sometime" in closing.

These are simply concluding words and are not a real invitation. The person receiving this pseudo-invitation should just say thank you and not expect that this plan will ever come to fruition. Pursuing the offer further would actually be a great imposition. It is important to remember that the function of the words is not an invitation. Rather, they are to conclude one topic and move to the next.

When refusing

If you're invited somewhere but don't want to go, you don't have to go into a lot of specifics. You can just say that you are busy that day, that the day is difficult for you, or that you have a prior commitment.

If you refuse once, Japanese people might hesitate to invite you again. **If you can't go that particular day but you'd like to go some other time you will need to add words to that effect,** for example, *Hontō ni zannen desu* (It's really a pity that I can't make it.) or *Mata sasotte kudasai* (Please invite me again.)

Invitations can be delicate negotiations but if you show your regret when refusing you can look forward to the next invitation.

G o o d *to* k n o w ······································

● よかったらどうぞ。[*Yokattara dōzo.*]
▷ Please come if you'd like.

● もしよていがはいっていなければ
[*moshi yotei ga haitte inakereba*]
▷ if you're not busy ...

● ぜひいらしてください。[*Zehi irashite kudasai.*]
▷ Please come.

● こんどいきましょう。[*Kondo ikimashō.*]
▷ Let's go sometime soon.

● あいにくそのひはいけません。
[*Ainiku sono hi wa ikemasen.*]
▷ Unfortunately, I can't go that day.

● そのひはようじがあります。
[*Sono hi wa yōji ga arimasu.*]
▷ I have a previous engagement that day.

● いそがしくていけません。[*Isogashikute ikemasen.*]
▷ I am busy that day.

● さそってくださってありがとうございます。
[*Sasotte kudasatte arigatō gozaimasu.*]
▷ Thank you for inviting me.

[頼む] *tanomu*

Requests

Can you help me?

Kevin Michaels' colleague, Tsuyoshi Sugiyama, came over to his desk one day and started explaining about a new project that he was working on. Kevin listened politely, adding comments like "That sounds like a good idea." After Sugiyama-*san* had talked for about five minutes he suddenly said to Kevin, "Can you help me with the project?" Kevin was taken aback. He hadn't realized Sugiyama-*san* was leading up to a request.

Lengthy prologues

Japanese people occasionally will say in advance that they have a request to make. But much more often **they will explain the situation in great detail before finally asking for help.** Although nothing is said about a request in advance, other Japanese people are usually aware that one will follow.

They know this because this kind of lengthy prologue is customary when asking a favor. **It can seem rude to ask for a favor without filling the person in on the background.** In addition, the prologue to the request is a good chance to appeal to the other person in terms of how important the project is and how

they really need the other person's assistance.

It is important to listen to the whole prologue even if you don't want to help. After that, you're free to accept or refuse as you see fit.

I'd like to help, but ...

If you are willing to help the person with the request, there's no problem. But if you need to say no, you should take care to refuse in a way that doesn't offend the other person. **A common strategy in Japan is to not completely refuse a request but rather to limit your involvement while still offering to do something.**

When you can't help at all, mentioning other work-related commitments works best. A typical way to refuse is "I'm pursued by work at the moment" or "I have a mountain of work right now." Of course, it's also nice to express regret at being unable to help.

Was a request made?

Sometimes you may think that someone has made a request of you when he or she didn't really mean it. This kind of misunderstanding usually stems from someone trying to be polite by making a vague suggestion of how you might be helpful, such as "Please let us know if you have any good ideas" or "Please help us."

Before envisioning your involvement in a full-scale project it's a good idea to make sure whether they are serious by asking for a few specifics. If you keep getting ambiguous responses they're probably just being polite.

On the other hand, you may not remember making a request but someone may suddenly behave as if they were fulfilling a request. What is going on here is that they probably perceived that you needed help (even if you think you're doing fine!) and decided on their own to pitch in.

In this situation the person is trying to be kind (see p.26 Consideration for Others). **You'll hurt the person's feelings if you say that you don't remember making a request.** Just thank him or her. After all, we all really do need a little help now and then.

G o o d *to* k n o w ·····································

- ●おねがいする［*onegai-suru*］
- ●たのむ［*tanomu*］
- ●おねがいできますか。［*Onegai dekimasu ka?*］
- ●できればおねがいしたいのですが。
  ［*Dekireba onegai-shitai no desu ga.*］
- ●いいですよ。［*Ii desu yo.*］
- ●ひきうける［*hikiukeru*］
- ●ことわる［*kotowaru*］
- ●おやくにたてなくてすみません。
  ［*Oyaku ni tatenakute sumimasen.*］
- ●いまはじかんのよゆうがありません。
  ［*Ima wa jikan no yoyū ga arimasen.*］

- ▷ make a request
- ▷ ask a favor
- ▷ Can I ask you to help?
- ▷ If possible, I'd like to ask for your help.

- ▷ Sure.
- ▷ agree to help
- ▷ refuse
- ▷ I'm sorry but I won't be able to be of use/assistance to you.
- ▷ I have no time available now.

Age Differences

How important is seniority?

sempai → kōhai

dōki ←→ dōki

Greg Bradford, a general manager at a large multinational, noticed his Japanese colleagues speaking respectfully to Akio Nakamura, a manager in another department of the same company. In terms of professional rank, Greg was higher, but Nakamura-*san* was about 55 and Greg was only 32. Greg wondered if he should show deference to Nakamura-*san* on the basis of his age.

Go ahead and pay respect

The short answer to Greg's dilemma is that yes, he should take care to be polite in this situation. Traditionally, Japanese people have venerated older people and placed great value on their experience. **Japanese companies are slowly becoming more merit-based but the old system of seniority still holds weight.**

In getting along with the Japanese it is important to be sensitive to age differences and to extend the proper courtesy. In particular, it is a good idea to avoid frank speech with older people.

Your intention may be friendly, but it can be perceived as boorishness and will cause the older person to lose face. Greg would be well advised to follow his col-league's tone as best as he can. **If you are careful to be polite to a person who is older, everyone will approve of your consideration.** As far as work itself goes, there is no need to defer to an older person's ideas simply because he or she is older.

Older brother or younger brother?

Age is also important in families. There is no generic word for brother or sister in Japanese, there are only the words older brother, *onīsan*, younger brother, *otōto*, older sister, *onēsan*, and younger sister, *imōto*. Even twins will be referred to based on who was born first. The younger twin will call the older twin *onīsan* or *onēsan*, rather than calling him or her by name.

Historically this was important in terms of inheritance. This is no longer generally the case but **the automatic labeling according to age points to the idea that Japanese people are more aware of age differences than Westerners.**

Experience over age

Schoolchildren refer to students who are one or more years ahead of them as *sempai*, senior, and those one or more years below as *kōhai*, junior. In these cases, age and experience correspond.

In companies, whoever has joined the company before you is your *sempai*. This is true even if, for example, you joined the company after graduate school and so are actually a few years older. What determines the relationship is years of experience at the company, not physical age or educational level.

***Sempai* are treated with esteem. In turn, *sempai* feel an obligation to watch out for their *kōhai*.** Then there are those who started work at exactly the same time as you. They are your *dōki* and you share a special relationship as equals.

These three patterns of relationships, *sempai-kōhai*, *kōhai-sempai*, and *dōki-dōki*, have great meaning for the Japanese. Paying attention to these seniority-based roles can be a way to bring your relationship with various people you work with to a deeper level.

G o o d *to* k n o w ·······································

- ●ねんれい [*nenrei*] ▷ a person's age
- ●としうえ [*toshiue*] ▷ older
- ●としした [*toshishita*] ▷ younger
- ●ねんぱいのかた [*nempai no kata*] ▷ an elderly person
- ●かめのこうよりとしのこう [*kame no kō yori toshi no kō*] ▷ literally, the wisdom (功), *kō*, of age is worth more than the shell (甲), *kō*, of a tortoise. This proverb, deriving from a play on words, is understood to emphasize the value of old age.
- ●そんけいをはらう [*sonkei o harau*] ▷ pay respect
- ●せんぱいぶる [*sempai-buru*] ▷ assume an air of seniority
- ●せんぱいにきく [*sempai ni kiku*] ▷ get advice from a veteran
- ●こうはいのめんどうをみる [*kōhai no mendō o miru*] ▷ take care of those less experienced

Getting Along with Friends

Are we buddies?

Susan Reece has been working for 10 months in Japan. She thinks she has several friends at work. They joke around together and sometimes go out after work. On the other hand, no one talks to her of personal problems unrelated to work, nor does she know if her closest colleague, Shingo Tomita, has a girlfriend. Are these really friends or just kind co-workers?

Conditions for friendship

As mentioned in "Inside and Outside," (see p.10) you will first be seen as an outsider in Japan. Gaining a closer relationship takes time. Also, Japanese people try to keep a clear-cut distinction between work and their personal lives. So even between Japanese friends who work together there will be less personal talk.

Susan is starting out as an outsider in a work-related setting, two things that make friendship more difficult. But in time, she will find real friends among her co-workers. Rather than focusing on how much personal stuff they reveal, she should ask herself which of her co-workers seem genuinely concerned at helping her cope with life's ups and downs. **In Japan, the definition of a friend is someone who you can rely on, not necessarily someone who confides in you.**

Gaining deep friendships

To get really close to someone you have to get away from the office. Try to find a chance to go out and talk about some things unrelated to work and you'll see another side of the person. **The more time you share together outside the office, the closer you'll become.** The aim is to get into a kind of relationship where you invite each other to various events and parties.

If you can't seem to get close to people you work with, it might be faster and more effective to try to find friendships elsewhere, for example, by joining some kind of club. Keep trying different approaches and different people and you're sure to make some good friends.

Points to heed

Japanese people are cautious about discussing private matters but if you are open they will open up to you in time, too. But there is a gap between what Japanese people and Western people mean by "open." **Japanese people are often very surprised by the readiness with which some non-Japanese will bare their souls to slight acquaintances.**

They will wait to see whether the person can be trusted before discussing anything personal. On top of that, private information is revealed on a need-to-know basis. It seems strange to the Japanese to discuss personal things just for the sake of discussing them.

It is very important to never tell anyone what someone has told you in confidence. If you do, you'll be labeled as a person who can't be trusted. Even if it's good news, keep your mouth shut. Each person wants to feel that they are in control of who knows what about them. For example, if Susan's friend Shingo tells her he's gotten engaged she should definitely not mention it to anyone.

If you become friends with a Japanese person they will consider you a friend for life, even if one of you changes jobs or moves away. **Japanese people are often hurt when a foreign friend returns to his or her home country and does not bother to keep up the connection.**

Take care of your friendships in Japan and you'll find that they may be some of the deepest you've ever had.

G o o d *to* k n o w ·

- ●ともだちがい [*tomodachigai*] ▷ true friendship
- ●まさかのともはしんのとも。 ▷ A friend in need is a friend indeed.
  [*Masaka no tomo wa shin no tomo.*]
- ●しんようできる [*shin'yō dekiru*] ▷ trustworthy
- ●しんゆう [*shin'yū*] ▷ a close friend
- ●うちとける [*uchitokeru*] ▷ open one's heart
- ●ボーイフレンド [*bōifurendo*] ▷ a friend who is male (not necessarily a boyfriend)
- ●ガールフレンド [*gārufurendo*] ▷ a friend who is female (not necessarily a girlfriend)
- ●こじんてきなはなし [*kojinteki na hanashi*] ▷ a personal matter

Getting Along with Neighbors

New kid on the block

When Beth and George Macy moved into a house in a suburb of Tokyo they were anxious to be on good relations with their neighbors. However, they were not sure how to accomplish this. Beth and George were not even sure of the neighbors' names and hoped that the neighbors would drop by to welcome them to the neighborhood. However, no one did.

We've just moved in

In America a neighbor might come over with a casserole or some baked cookies to say hello. In Japan, the neighbors are waiting for you. **When new people move into a neighborhood in Japan they usually buy a small gift such as soap or hand towels for each of the families in the vicinity.** Then they go around to each house introducing themselves. It is up to you to make the first move.

What goes on in this preliminary meeting? You probably will not be invited in (and in fact you may live side by side with a neighbor for years and never see their living room.) You will present your gift and explain your name and a little more information such as where you moved from.

In turn, the neighbor will welcome you and give you some advice about the area. **A frequently proffered piece of information is about the garbage collection schedule. This is vital knowledge since failure to follow the rules is a major cause of residential friction.** If you live in a condominium, the so-called *manshon*, there may be additional regulations governing communal areas.

Neighborhood association

Neighbors in Japan are usually cordial but not overly friendly. **Your main tie with them will probably be through the neighborhood association, or** *chōnaikai.* The *chōnaikai* is responsible for coordinating all community-related events and monthly fees are collected from all residents.

An autumn festival is usually a major event planned by the neighborhood association and in many cases, both adults and children participate. The children eat cotton candy, catch goldfish, and play games for prizes while the adults who are not helping with the festival enjoy the chance to see their neighbors.

Information is usually conveyed via a *kairamban*, a clipboard with announcements attached to it that is passed from house to house. Apartment or condominium residents don't use *kairamban* but notices are usually posted in a designated place in the building.

The *kairamban* or notices will let you know things like when a community festival is to be held, information about neighbors' wakes and funerals, or if street construction is planned.

Adding a layer of warmth

As long as you follow the community's rules and observe common sense in terms of not playing music too loud, etc., you'll be fine. When neighbors run into each other on the street they usually greet each other or may add a comment or two about the weather.

It's a good idea to try to find one person in the area who can give you information about what's going on. This can be a restaurant or shop owner as well as a resident. Participating in any community events can also create a nice feeling. A neighborly feeling, in fact.

G o o d *to* **k n o w** ······································

- ●きんじょ [*kinjo*]
  ▷ a neighborhood
- ●このきんじょにひっこしてきました。
  [*Kono kinjo ni hikkoshite kimashita.*]
  ▷ We just moved into this neighborhood.
- ●きんじょづきあい [*kinjo-zukiai*]
  ▷ getting along with neighbors
- ●となりのひと [*tonari no hito*]
  ▷ a next-door neighbor
- ●きんじょめいわく [*kinjo-meiwaku*]
  ▷ a neighborhood nuisance
- ●ごみのひ [*gomi no hi*]
  ▷ a garbage day
- ●かいらんばんをまわす
  [*kairamban o mawasu*]
  ▷ pass on the *kairamban* announcement clipboard
- ●…です [*... desu*]
  ▷ I'm ...
- ●…からきました [*... kara kimashita*]
  ▷ I moved here from ...

Going Out to Eat

How are things done at restaurants?

Brenda Lewis went out to an Italian restaurant with some female colleagues after work. When the waitress came to take their orders Brenda told her what she wanted. But after that, the rest of the colleagues ordered a number of dishes to eat together. Brenda worried that she had been rude and she felt kind of silly when her order arrived and was placed in front of her while other dishes were placed in the middle of the table for everyone to eat.

Ordering patterns

When women go out together they often like to order together and share the dishes. If you'd rather not, there's nothing wrong with ordering something on your own. Groups of men tend to wait for whoever is of higher rank to order first. Then they order the same thing or something a little cheaper. In either case, you don't have to hurry to order. **See what everyone else is thinking about ordering and take it from there.**

Vegetarian foreigners sometimes ask for dishes to be modified but that's just not done in Japan and the restaurant invariably won't comply if asked. However, there are usually things to order with no meat in them, so it is a good idea to choose from what is available.

Who's paying?

Japanese people will often treat others if the restaurant is near their own office or home as a way of thanking the person for coming over, if they have a higher position, or if they want to celebrate something or thank the other person. **When colleagues go out together in a large group they usually split the check, *warikan*.**

But in small groups, people often treat each other to meals, especially if there is some reason for celebration. **Treating and being treated is seen as a way of becoming friends.** In addition, some people find the practice of asking for separate checks unattractive. Some Japanese men feel uncomfortable allowing a woman to pay for herself. You generally don't need to worry that because they paid for you they have a hidden agenda.

In almost all restaurants, including expensive ones, you pay at the front rather than at the table. If someone else announces that they will pay, it is considered good manners to move away from the cash register so you can't see the money transaction take place.

When the person joins you after paying you say *Gochisōsama deshita*, "Thank you for the meal/drink." You say this again when you say your final goodbyes that day.

Another party?

When the get-together is a party, the group, or at least part of it, will usually move on to another bar or coffee shop for a second, more informal, party, or *niji-kai,* after the first main party has finished. **Parties rarely end at the time announced.** That is simply the timetable for making the move to the next place.

People in higher positions usually don't go on to the *niji-kai*. Often on top of the *niji-kai* there will be a third party, called a *sanji-kai*. **Gradually, the group thins out, leaving the core members.** The official party was a formality; the real communication takes place later. So if you go to the *niji-kai* you'll have an even more interesting experience. Party on!

G o o d *to* k n o w ·

- ●なににしましょうか。[*Nani ni shimashō ka?*] ▷ What shall we eat?
- ●…がにがてです。[*... ga nigate desu.*] ▷ I can't eat ...
- ●おごります。[*Ogorimasu.*] ▷ It's my treat.
- ●ごちそうする [*gochisō-suru*] ▷ treat a person
- ●ごちそうになる [*gochisō ni naru*] ▷ be treated
- ●わりかんにする [*warikan ni suru*] ▷ split the check
- ●べつべつでおねがいします。 ▷ Separate checks, please.
  [*Betsubetsu de onegai-shimasu.*]
- ●にじかい [*niji-kai*] ▷ a second party
- ●かんじ [*kanji*] ▷ a person in charge of organizing a party

Gift-Giving Seasons

Why am I getting this?

ochūgen

oseibo

In early December Chuck Rogers, an advertising executive, opened a box addressed to him at his office. Inside it were 12 cans of juice. There was no card attached but the return address indicated that it was from Shigeru Saito, someone at a printing company that his company has used. Why in the world was Saito-*san* sending him juice?

Two times for presents

Japan has two important gift-giving periods. *Ochūgen* is at the beginning of July. It is followed by *oseibo*, at the beginning of December. Of the two, *oseibo* is more important. During these gift-giving seasons, department stores have special areas set up specifically for the selling of these gifts.

The presents are wrapped in paper from the department store and a long strip of white paper with the word お中元 (*ochūgen*) or お歳暮 (*oseibo*) written vertically is attached. These gifts are usually sent directly from the department store, although they may also be delivered by the giver in person if you wish.

Christmas or birthday presents are rare in the workplace.

These gift-giving seasons are a time to show appreciation to those who have helped you in some way. The presents can be sent from one person to another or from one company to another.

Down-to-up focus

While in Western countries many bosses give their subordinates Christmas presents and so on, **the directional focus of Japanese gift-giving is generally from down to up.**

Companies send out many seasonal gifts to their clients. Sometimes these are sent in the name of one person to a specific person, as in Chuck's case, and sometimes the company as a whole may send a present to another company or department of another company.

On a personal level, people give presents to those to whom they have a debt of gratitude, *onjin*, or who have provided them with some kind of assistance, for example, by employing them. These include bosses, teachers, doctors, landlords, the go-between at their wedding, and sometimes relatives who live elsewhere.

Gifts of food common

The gifts are usually very impersonal and basic. Articles for consumption are most common. Coffee, ham, canned fruit, *nori* (dried seaweed), pickles, butter, green tea, soap, towels and cooking oil are some typical gift choices.

When sending a gift to the office, people usually send something the whole staff can enjoy, like rice crackers, cookies, chocolates, beer or juice. **It is entirely acceptable to send the same thing year after year.**

If you receive *ochūgen* or *oseibo* **it is ordinarily not necessary to reciprocate** but if a specific person is mentioned on the return address it is nice to thank them in person, by phone or via a short card.

If someone has helped you during the year, this is a great chance to show your gratitude by trying a tradition enjoyed by many Japanese people.

Good to know

- おくりもの [*okurimono*] ▷ a present
- おかえし [*okaeshi*] ▷ a present in return
- おちゅうげん・おせいぼうりば [*ochūgen/oseibo-uriba*] ▷ a sales area for *ochūgen/oseibo*
- のしがみ [*noshigami*] ▷ a strip of paper attached to a present
- このじゅうしょにおくってください。[*Kono jūsho ni okutte kudasai.*] ▷ Please send it to this address.
- いつもおせわになっています。[*Itsumo osewa ni natte imasu.*] ▷ Thank you for all your help. (said when giving an *ochūgen* or *oseibo* present in person)
- ありがたくちょうだいします。[*Arigataku chōdai-shimasu.*] ▷ I accept your present with gratitude. (said when receiving an *ochūgen* or *oseibo* present in person)
- すてきなプレゼントをありがとうございました。[*Sutekina purezento o arigatō gozaimashita.*] ▷ Thank you for the wonderful present. (said or written after a present has been sent to you)

Gifts for Special Occasions

What are those envelopes?

Adam French was invited to the wedding reception of his colleague, Mitsuru Takahashi. As a wedding gift he brought a large ceramic salad bowl made by potters in his native state of Vermont. However, when he arrived at the wedding reception he noticed each guest handed a beautiful envelope to a person at a table near the entrance and no one seemed to have brought a present. Adam thought, "Oops!"

Monetary gifts

People do sometimes send wedding presents but **those invited to a wedding reception usually bring money.** Most Japanese people feel that money is the best choice because the person receiving it can use it as they like.

Money given on happy occasions is placed in a special white envelope with a red and white or gold tie, called a *noshi-bukuro*, which is sold at stationery stores. Typical joyful events for which money or a present may be given include marriage and the birth of a child.

They also include some events not necessarily commemorated with presents in the West, for example, reaching age 20 (the legal age of adulthood in Japan), joining a company or entering a school.

Children are given money in little envelopes at the New Year, called *oto-shidama*. This New Year's money is looked forward to as eagerly as Christmas presents or birthday presents.

Money is given in sorrowful circumstances, too. Money presented to the bereaved upon the death of a family member is called *kōden*. The envelope has a black and white or silver tie. Money is also sometimes given in cases of illness, fire or earthquake. This is known as *omimai*. A regular envelope can be used or a special one that is white with a red border and no tie.

It's all in the presentation

The money is placed in another thin envelope inside the main envelope (the envelopes are sold as a set) and the amount of money contained is written on the backside of the envelope along with the name of the person giving the money. Notes are usually not enclosed. **Especially on happy occasions, it is considered important that the bills be crisp and new** so people often go to the bank to get brand-new money.

Presents or money envelopes are given and received with both hands. Using just one hand violates etiquette.

Traditionally, Japanese people do not open a gift in the presence of the giver. But recently, if the people are friends, the person receiving the present may sometimes open it on the spot. Care is taken when opening a gift not to tear the wrapping paper. Ripping open a present is seen as evidence that you are a person of rough manners, not that you are enthusiastic about the present.

Gifts in return

It is customary to make a present in return after receiving one on a special occasion. This is called *okaeshi*. It is a way of acknowledging and reciprocating the goodwill expressed by the gift-giver. All guests at wedding receptions receive a lavish present as they leave, for example.

Funeral guests receive a small present as they leave. In addition, they are later sent another present equivalent to about half of the money received. This is called *han-gaeshi*, giving half in return. The custom of *han-gaeshi* is also followed after receiving presents in cases of a birth, illness, fire or earthquake.

G o o d *to* k n o w ······································

- ●みずひき [*mizuhiki*]
- ●けっこんいわい [*kekkon-iwai*]
- ●しゅっさんいわい [*shussan-iwai*]
- ●にゅうがくいわい [*nyūgaku-iwai*]
- ●みまいきん [*mimai-kin*]

- ●うちいわい [*uchi-iwai*]

- ●つまらないものですが…。
  [*Tsumaranai mono desu ga ...*]
- ●あけてもいいでしょうか。
  [*Aketemo ii deshō ka?*]

▷ a tie on a money envelope
▷ a wedding present
▷ a gift in celebration of a birth
▷ a gift in celebration of entering a school
▷ money given in case of illness, fire or earthquake
▷ a gift given by a family to celebrate their own happy event
▷ This is something plain but ... (a humble set phrase used when giving a gift)
▷ May I open it?

Greeting Cards

I hope you're not too hot!

Larry Thomas received a postcard in July from a business acquaintance. It read, "It has become very hot. Please take care of yourself." A few days later Larry received a postcard from yet another associate with the words, "How are you getting along in these hot days?" Four more such cards followed. The Japanese summer was certainly steamy but Larry wondered why so many people were showing such concern.

Health inquiries

Japanese people send postcards in the summer and at New Year's. New Year's is the main time for sending cards but most people receive at least a few summer cards as well.

The summer cards inquire after a person's health and are of two types depending on when they are sent. *Shochū-mimai* cards are sent from July to August 7th and *zansho-mimai* cards from August 8th until the end of August.

The postcards are often government-issued ones sold through the post office with a lottery number printed at the bottom. If you receive a card it is nice to send a note in return saying thank you.

Happy New Year!

New Year's cards, or *nenga-jō*, are a very important and fun tradition in Japan, similar to Christmas cards in the West. The cards usually give a wee bit of information about what has been going on in the life of the sender and his or her family over the past year. They also express wishes for a good relationship with the addressee in the year ahead. Companies send out official cards with a brief report about the state of the business.

Most people print or create their own cards on plain white postcards or, again, on blank ones featuring printed lottery numbers on the face and sold through the post office.

Printers usually have a variety of designs available, to which the sender's name and address can be added. It is also possible to have cards printed with a photograph of the family. **The cards often have a picture of whatever animal is associated with that year according to the traditional twelve-year cycle.**

When writing the addressee's name and address it is considered permissible to use a word processor but the card should include some handwritten message.

Not before January 1st

The Japanese speak of the New Year "opening." Until it "opens," it is therefore "closed" and **it would be very strange to receive a New Year's card before January 1st.**

People sending New Year's cards put a rubber band around them, inserting a piece of paper on top that identifies them as New Year's cards. **The cards are put in a special, designated post slot at the post office or mailboxes and held by the post office until the New Year.**

On New Year's Day when the cards arrive, the whole family looks through them, enjoying the various designs and messages. People keep the cards sent to them for reference when sending cards out the following year.

New Year's cards are the Japanese tradition, but if you send Christmas cards to your Japanese friends and acquaintances instead, they will be delighted to receive them. The form may be different, but the good wishes conveyed are the same.

G o o d *to* k n o w ·····································

● しょちゅうおみまいもうしあげます。
  [*Shochū-omimai mōshi-agemasu.*]

● ざんしょおみまいもうしあげます。
  [*Zansho-omimai mōshi-agemasu.*]

● あけましておめでとうございます。
  [*Akemashite omedetō gozaimasu.*]

● げいしゅん（迎春）[*geishun*]

● きんがしんねん（謹賀新年）
  [*kinga-shinnen*]

● ことしもよろしくおねがいします。
  [*Kotoshi mo yoroshiku onegai-shimasu.*]

● もちゅうにつき、ねんまつねんしのごあい
  さつをごえんりょもうしあげます。
  [*Mochū ni tsuki nemmatsu-nenshi no goaisatsu
  o goenryo mōshi-agemasu.*]

▷ I inquire about your health in the middle of summer.

▷ I inquire about your health in the lingering heat.

▷ Happy New Year! (spoken as well as written on New Year's cards)

▷ Welcome, spring (written on New Year's cards)

▷ Happy New Year (written on New Year's cards)

▷ I look forward to our continuing good relationship in the year ahead.

▷ Being in mourning I won't be sending New Year's greetings. (the message on postcards sent in early December by those who have had a death in the family during the year)

67

Visiting Others' Homes

Hospitality puzzles

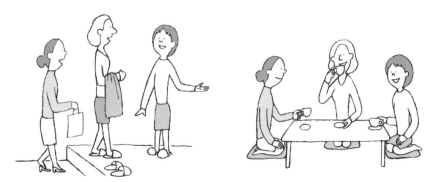

Sandra Black and her colleagues Chieko Furuya and Junko Ishida were discussing a software program that Ishida-*san* had installed on her computer at home. Ishida-*san* suggested that Sandra and Furuya-*san* come by on Saturday afternoon to try it out for themselves. When Sandra and Furuya-*san* met at the station to walk there, Sandra was surprised to see that Furuya-*san* had brought a big box of cookies with her while she herself hadn't thought to bring anything. Was Sandra being rude?

Visiting with gifts

When a Japanese person pays a social call to the home of another they usually bring a small present, called an *omiyage* or *temiyage*, such as some cookies or flowers, even if they do not expect to eat a meal there. To visit someone in Japanese is called *ojama-suru*, literally to "bother" someone. Bringing a gift is a way of acknowledging the imposition. You should probably pick something up on your way to someone's house.

If you're unexpectedly invited or you just plain forgot to bring an *omiyage*, you can apologize by saying, *Tebura de sumimasen* (Sorry for being empty-handed.)

Come on up!

People don't enter another's house as freely as they do in the West. At the entranceway, or *genkan*, the person whose house it is will say, *Dōzo oagari kudasai*. This means "Please come up." This is because the main part of the house is higher up than the *genkan*.

Remove your coat and shoes while in the *genkan*, arranging the shoes neatly. You'll probably be given some slippers to wear inside the house. If you're shown to a Japanese-style room, take off the slippers before stepping onto the *tatami* straw mats. The host will give you a cushion, called a *zabuton*, to sit on. It's considered good manners to sit formally until told to relax. You can give your *omiyage* to them now.

All visitors to a home are usually served some kind of beverage and possibly some cookies or rice crackers. You should wait to eat and drink until the host says, *Dōzo* (Go ahead.) Then say *Itadakimasu* (Thank you for the food/drink) before partaking.

People in the West often show guests around the house but **in Japan other rooms are considered private so you probably won't be shown them and it's not a good idea to ask for a tour.**

Time for goodbye

After you announce that you have to leave, don't be surprised if no one urges you to stay longer. It can even seem like you may have outstayed your welcome because your coat will be brought to you very speedily. But don't worry. Partings just tend to progress faster in Japan. So **while in the West you might say "Well, I should be going ..." about fifteen minutes before you actually intend to leave, in Japan you can just wait until right before you plan on exiting** to say, *Soro soro*, the Japanese equivalent.

Japanese people usually escort guests out of the house and stand and watch them until they are out of sight. **It can feel strange to know that someone is watching your back as you walk away but the intention is to see you safely off.** Right before you disappear from vision it is nice to turn around and wave one final time. Bye-bye!

G o o d *to* **k n o w** ･･････････････････････････････

● おみやげ・てみやげ [*omiyage/temiyage*] ▷ a present brought to someone's home or company

● どうぞおかまいなく。[*Dōzo okamainaku.*] ▷ Please don't go to any trouble.

● もてなし [*motenashi*] ▷ hospitality

● ほうもん [*hōmon*] ▷ a visit

● ホームパーティ [*hōmu pātī*] ▷ a party at a person's home

● みおくる [*miokuru*] ▷ see a person off

● きをつけてください。[*Ki o tsukete kudasai.*] ▷ Take care!

● おじゃましました。[*Ojama-shimashita.*] ▷ Thank you for inviting me. (literally, "I bothered you.")

Eating at People's Homes

From plate to mouth

Tom Starr was invited for dinner to the house of his colleague, Hiroshi Matsuda. Tom had eaten often at Japanese restaurants but this was the first time for him to eat in a Japanese person's home and he could tell it was a big deal for the Matsudas. He didn't want to offend them by doing something wrong, but he suddenly realized he didn't really know that much about food etiquette, especially in the case of communal dishes.

Communal food

When everyone is assembled at the table and the food is served, Japanese people say *Itadakimasu*, which means "We receive the food." After that, you can start eating. **There are usually a variety of dishes served but there is no special order in which to eat them.**

You probably won't be given a napkin but you may be given an *oshibori*, a damp towel to wipe your hands with. If the meal is served in a room with *tatami* straw mats and it's hard for you to sit the traditional Japanese style with your feet tucked under, you may find a more comfortable position.

Food on large plates is often passed around and each person takes their por-

tion. **If there is no serving utensil, you are supposed to use the other end of your chopsticks to take the food,** then turn your chopsticks around to eat. This keeps your germs away from the food other people will eat. However, if you're eating something like *sukiyaki* where you take food a little bit at a time rather than one portion all at once, you can use your chopsticks the right end round.

It is considered bad manners to hover around the food indecisively looking for the choicest morsel. **Before you go near the plate with your chopsticks, decide what you're aiming for and get it onto your plate as quickly as possible.**

Busy hands

Your hands will not be hidden under the table. Rather, they should be active throughout the meal. **When eating rice or drinking soup using chopsticks you will hold the bowl in your left hand as you take the food with your chopsticks in your right hand** (assuming you are right-handed).

Most of the time during the meal you will be holding your rice bowl as you pick up other pieces of food. This is because you will often be eating the food together with the rice. Also, having the rice bowl suspended midway between the table and your mouth is useful in case you drop something en route. It is good manners to eat all of your rice and other food.

Relax and enjoy the meal

These are the big differences. The rest is mostly common sense: compliment the cook, eat what is served to you, and try not to be too messy. **It is not impolite to make a certain amount of noise when consuming a hot liquid such as miso soup or green tea.** If you're not sure what to do, watch what the others are doing, or just go ahead and ask.

The best thing you can do is show your appreciation for the effort that has been made by relaxing and enjoying the meal. When you finish eating, you should say *Gochisōsama* (Thank you for the delightful meal.) or *Oishikatta desu* (It was delicious.) Bon appétit!

G o o d *to* **k n o w** ························

- ●おはし [*ohashi*]
- ●まよいばし [*mayoi-bashi*]
- ●おしぼり [*oshibori*]
- ●あしをくずす [*ashi o kuzusu*]
- ●とりざら [*torizara*]
- ●おかわり [*okawari*]
- ●おいしいです。[*Oishii desu.*]
- ●おなかがいっぱいです。
  [*Onaka ga ippai desu.*]

- ▷ chopsticks
- ▷ hovering chopsticks
- ▷ a damp towel for wiping hands
- ▷ sit at ease
- ▷ a saucer to put food on
- ▷ another helping/serving
- ▷ This is delicious.
- ▷ I'm full.

Going Out Drinking

What's the pub experience all about?

Brad Green is occasionally invited to go out drinking with various colleagues. Because Brad doesn't like to drink, he has turned down the invitations so far. However, he knows that going out drinking is a big part of the Japanese business culture and wonders whether he's going to lose out if he doesn't join in.

An opportunity to relax

The point in going out drinking in Japan is not really the drinking itself. **Businesspeople see it as an opportunity to relax and get to know each other away from the office.** This can be a really good chance to ask about anything that has been puzzling you at work.

There are a range of types of drinking establishments, from some tiny bars that seat no more than 10 customers at teeny-weeny tables, to large pubs with low tables set on *tatami* straw mats where large groups can spread out.

It is unusual to just have a quick one and go home. Going out drinking is a full evening's entertainment and people frequently go bar-hopping. Some people look forward to putting away a few or more and **it is socially acceptable to get fairly drunk.** Others drink moderately and some abstain. Those who do not drink alcohol usually drink cold oolong tea or orange juice.

More than drinking

A lot of healthy eating also takes place. **The Japanese almost never drink without eating something.** You may occasionally see peanuts but you are much more likely to eat a lot of tofu, vegetable and fish dishes. These are usually substantial enough to constitute a dinner.

Karaoke is also sometimes a part of the drinking experience. Some bars have karaoke equipment and various people sing in front of all the customers, who may also join in on the refrains. Other times people go to "karaoke boxes," purpose-built establishments with small karaoke rooms where your group can drink, eat and sing in privacy.

Japanese people like to sing as well as listen to others sing. There are plenty of both English and Japanese songs. **Don't worry if you're tone deaf — they'll love whatever wavering notes you manage.** If you're a born performer, now's your chance to really ham it up.

Keep those glasses filled!

It is common etiquette to fill each other's glasses and to keep topping each other off so they never get empty. When another person fills your glass it is good manners to hold the glass as they do so.

Sometimes Japanese people urge others rather forcefully to drink and go ahead pouring you beer or sake despite your protests. What you may see as overbearing is their way of being friendly, particularly since it is polite to decline such an offer even if in reality you want to drink. If you don't want to drink what they've poured you, just leave it in the glass since if your glass is full your counterpart can't pour any more anyway.

It is usually considered impolite to fill your own glass. You should wait until someone else notices your glass is empty and let them fill it. Generally, if you fill another person's glass they will return the favor by filling yours. Cheers!

| G | o | o | d | *to* | k | n | o | w |

●のみにいく ［*nomi ni iku*］ ▷ go drinking

●いっぱいやる ［*ippai yaru*］ ▷ have a drink

●のみや ［*nomiya*］ ▷ a drinking establishment

●いざかや ［*izakaya*］ ▷ a Japanese-style pub

●さけ ［*sake*］ ▷ alcohol

●にほんしゅ ［*nihonshu*］ ▷ Japanese sake

●とっくり ［*tokkuri*］ ▷ a sake pitcher

●おちょこ ［*ochoko*］ ▷ a sake cup

tokkuri   ochoko

●さけのさかな・おつまみ ［*sake no sakana/otsumami*］ ▷ food to eat while drinking

●さけによわい ［*sake ni yowai*］ ▷ (a person who) becomes tipsy quickly

●さけにつよい ［*sake ni tsuyoi*］ ▷ (one who) can hold his/her liquor well

●のみすぎ ［*nomisugi*］ ▷ drink too much

●よっぱらう ［*yopparau*］ ▷ become drunk

Really, Really Good to Know

Getting by with 10 expressions

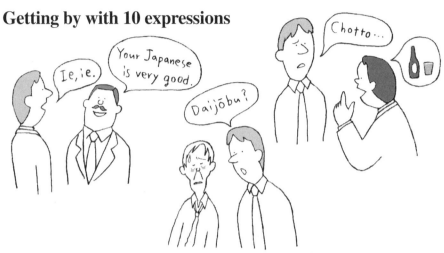

Stanley Lowell doesn't know a lot of Japanese. In fact, he only knows 10 expressions. When Japanese people hear this they are very surprised because they were sure Stanley knew a lot more. This is because these 10 expressions get Stanley through many situations he encounters. Here is a day in the life of our hero.

Stanley goes to work and is introduced to a new client. He says, ***Dōzo yoroshiku onegai-shimasu.*** ❶ The client says his Japanese is very good and Stanley replies modestly, ***Ie, ie.*** ❷ The client goes on to explain about his company. At regular intervals Stanley expresses his interest by saying ***Sō desu ka?*** ❸ After the meeting, Stanley's boss tells him what he'd like Stanley to do in terms of follow-up and Stanley says, ***Wakarimashita.*** ❹

On his way back to his desk he passes by his colleague, Ryohei Kawada, who looks exhausted and depressed. Stanley, concerned, asks, ***Daijōbu?*** ❺ Kawada-*san* tells him that he's been working day and night on a proposal that he has to submit tomorrow. Stanley encourages him by saying ***Gambatte!*** ❻

Later that day, another colleague, Jin Akiyama, drops by Stanley's desk to ask him to go out drinking that night. Stanley looks troubled and says ***Chotto ...*** ❼

Stanley has been invited to the home of his friend Michio Hara and his wife Sachiko. As he steps inside their house, he accidentally knocks over an umbrella propped against the wall. He apologizes, saying, ***Sumimasen.*** ❽

Stanley and the Haras have a nice meal together. When Mrs. Hara offers him a second cup of coffee, Stanley indicates he has had enough by saying ***Kekkō desu.*** ❾ As he leaves he says, ***Dōmo arigatō.*** ❿ Stanley goes home and gets a good night's sleep, ready for whatever lies ahead of him the next day.

Good *to* know ···

❶ *Dōzo yoroshiku onegai-shimasu* （どうぞよろしくおねがいします） literally means "Please be nice to me." It is used when meeting a person for the first time. It is also a useful closing to a conversation, suggesting that you look forward to a continuing good relationship with that person.

❷ *Ie, ie* （いえ、いえ） means "No, no." It is often used to brush off compliments. People often use it after being thanked for something, in which case it means something like "Not at all."

❸ *Sō desu ka?* （そうですか？） means "Is that so?" Depending on the intonation you can use it to express real surprise. When spoken more neutrally, it shows polite interest. People sometimes use it when complimented in order to express modest disbelief.

❹ *Wakarimashita* （わかりました） means "I understand." Subordinates use it to their bosses as a way to show that they accept an assignment. It is also used to sum up a conversation with the implication that the time for words has finished and the speaker will now move on to acting on the ideas expressed.

❺ *Daijōbu?* （だいじょうぶ？） here means "Are you OK?" It can be used when someone seems troubled or to show consternation if, for example, you bump into someone. It can also mean "Is it OK?" and you can use it to confirm that some arrangements are all right. With people you don't know it is more polite to say *Daijōbu desu ka?*

❻ *Gambatte!* （がんばって！） means "Hang in there!" but it functions in much the same way that "Good luck!" does in English. Whenever people speak of any plans it is usual for the other person to say *Gambatte!* (see p.23 Diligence)

❼ *Chotto ...* （ちょっと…） literally means "It's a little ..." Depending on the context this can mean many things but it is basically used to indicate a negative response. It can be used to turn down a request or invitation, meaning "It's a little difficult or inconvenient for me."

❽ *Sumimasen* （すみません） is a casual apology. It can also be used as a light thank you, for example, if someone brings you a cup of tea, or to get someone's attention, like "Excuse me." (see p.46 Apologizing)

❾ *Kekkō desu* （けっこうです） is used to refuse something that has been offered. It is a definite "no" so Stanley didn't use it when invited to go drinking with Jin because it would sound too strong. But it's often used to turn down food. It is also used to refuse unsolicited offers, for example, telephone sales calls.

❿ *Dōmo arigatō* （どうもありがとう） means "Thank you very much." Whenever someone does something for you, you can use this to express your appreciation. In casual situations *Arigatō* is enough. (see p.44 Expressing Gratitude)

Important Life Events

Meeting Someone and Getting Engaged

How are arranged marriages arranged?

Rudy Peterson recently got to know a colleague named Jun Sawada. One night they went out drinking and talked about their families. Rudy asked Sawada-*san* how he first met his wife and Sawada-*san* replied that it was an arranged marriage. Rudy was surprised and wanted to know more but didn't want to pry. Still he wondered what arranged marriage entailed.

Mediating marriage

In Japan there are two types of marriages, *miai kekkon*, arranged marriages, and *ren'ai kekkon*, love marriages. This seems to imply that love is not a part of arranged marriages, but **most people believe that an arranged meeting is a chance to meet someone who you might fall in love with and end up marrying.**

Arranged marriages continue to be popular. In general it is felt that the system is a good way for people who are well suited to meet. While parents may root for a particular candidate it is by no means compulsory to go along with parents' wishes.

The meetings are usually arranged by a mutual acquaintance. Some women enjoy introducing men and women. They often have data on many young people and thrive on the challenge of finding the perfect match.

Other times, friends or older members of the person's company may introduce potential partners and arrange the meeting. Recently, there are also marriage arrangement companies, which are similar to computer dating services, although the clear emphasis is on finding a compatible companion for life.

Finding Mr./Ms. Right

When men and women reach an age that is considered a good age to marry, they are likely to be approached by family members or acquaintances inquiring whether they'd like to give arranged marriage a try.

If they are interested, **the man or woman will give the go-between a picture of themselves and their resume. This resume often includes basic facts about their family, information about their hopes for the future, their income, height, weight and a description of their personality.** If there is anything they want to know about a potential marriage candidate they will include that as well.

Then the person will be shown similar information about possible mates. **If both sides express an interest, a meeting will be set up.**

If both say OK

After the meeting, the two people will each let the go-between know if they'd like to see the other person again. The go-between will relay the response to the other. **As meetings proceed, if at any time one person decides that they want to stop the relationship, they will express this via the go-between.** If a proposal is made and accepted, the go-between will be informed.

If a proposal is put forth and accepted, the next step is a formal engagement meeting, called *yuinō*. The couple and their families will meet and the engagement ring will be given to the bride-to-be.

Traditionally betrothal gifts are also exchanged. Practices differ depending on region, but **in some cases the groom-to-be gives his intended two to three months' salary in cash,** which helps to pay for the wedding. With this, they've completed the first step on the way to the wedding vows.

G o o d *to* **k n o w** ·······································

- ●おみあいしゃしん［*omiai-shashin*］ ▷ a photograph to be used for arranging marriages
- ●しょうかいしゃ［*shōkai-sha*］ ▷ someone who introduces two people
- ●えんだん［*endan*］ ▷ a proposal for meeting with the possibility of marriage
- ●えんだんをことわる ▷ refuse the possibility of marriage
  ［*endan o kotowaru*］
- ●けっこんをもうしこむ ▷ make a marriage proposal
  ［*kekkon o mōshikomu*］
- ●こんやくする［*kon'yaku-suru*］ ▷ become engaged
- ●こんやくゆびわ［*kon'yaku-yubiwa*］ ▷ an engagement ring
- ●ゆいのう［*yuinō*］ ▷ an exchange of betrothal gifts

Weddings

How do people tie the knot in Japan?

Mark Whitman received an invitation to the wedding reception of his colleague, Eiki Yamakura. He was surprised to see that he was invited to the reception but not to the ceremony. He was also surprised that his wife had not been invited. He wondered what to expect on the big day.

Private vows

In Japan, the wedding ceremony and reception are often separate. **Usually, only family members and very close friends attend the wedding ceremony.** The reception is bigger but spouses of friends or colleagues are not often invited unless they are personal acquaintances of the bride or groom.

Traditionally, weddings are Shinto rites. In Shinto wedding ceremonies, the bride wears a white long outer garment called an *uchikake* on top of a white kimono. She also wears a piece of white silk covering her head. The idea is that her face is concealed until the wedding ceremony is over. The groom wears a black kimono and gray *hakama* trousers.

After a wedding chant by the Shinto priest, the bride and groom drink Japanese sake three times each out of three successively bigger cups in a ritual known as *sansan-kudo.*

Recently, Christian weddings are also popular. Some Japanese women want to wear a Western wedding dress even if they do not consider themselves Christian. A final type of wedding is called *jinzen*. In *jinzen* weddings, secular wedding vows are exchanged in front of all the guests.

Seated receptions

Wedding receptions usually take place at hotels or wedding halls. The bride and groom sit at a separate head table in front, facing the guests, along with the *nakōdo*, also known as *baishakunin*. **The *nakōdo* are a married couple that serve the role of the marriage facilitators or go-betweens.** If the marriage is an arranged marriage this couple may have actually been the matchmakers, but not necessarily. Usually, the groom's boss and his wife do the honors.

The rest of the guests sit at assigned tables and usually eat a full-course meal. **There is very little walking around and no dancing.** Various people give speeches and some people may sing a song. Part of the way through the reception, the bride and groom move from table to table lighting candles at each. This gives the guests a chance to congratulate the couple.

Entering the family register

Legally, the marriage takes place when either the bride or groom (usually the bride) enters the other's family register, or *koseki*. This means that he or she is now a member of the family as a spouse. By entering the family register they assume the family name.

Because the number of children per family is declining, families with no sons to carry on the family name are increasing. Thus, more and more people want to have separate last names after marriage, but according to current Japanese law, a married couple must officially have the same last name.

It is not considered very important whether the couple enters the name in the family register before or after the wedding ceremony and reception. Some couples may do it as much as several weeks before or after. The main event is the public recognition that two families have been joined through marriage.

G o o d *to* **k n o w** ···

- ●けっこんしき　[*kekkon-shiki*]　▷a wedding ceremony
- ●ひろうえん　[*hirōen*]　▷a wedding reception
- ●はなよめ　[*hanayome*]　▷a bride
- ●はなむこ　[*hanamuko*]　▷a groom
- ●しんろうしんぷ　[*shinrō-shimpu*]　▷a bride and groom
- ●おめでとうございます。　▷Congratulations!
  [*Omedetō gozaimasu.*]
- ●しんこんりょこう　[*shinkon-ryokō*]　▷a honeymoon
- ●にゅうせき　[*nyūseki*]　▷being added to a family register
- ●ふうふ　[*fūfu*]　▷a married couple

Wedding Q&A

What are they doing and what am I supposed to do?

Vicky Roberts received an invitation to a colleague's wedding reception. She didn't want to do anything embarrassing or rude by accident. She thought she'd feel more comfortable and enjoy herself more if she studied up a bit before attending.

Q I received an invitation to a wedding reception. How should I respond?

A It is important to send out your response quickly. The couple to be married will use this information in planning the seating arrangements. As in the illustration above, you will circle whether you plan to attend (出席; *shusseki*) or be absent (欠席; *kesseki*) and write your name and address. It is customary to show modesty by crossing out the honorific 御、お and/or ご in front of all information pertaining to you. It is nice to add a short message of congratulations on the card.

Q Why do people usually give money instead of wedding presents?

A Japan in general has a tradition of giving money on special occasions. On top of this, the money is seen as a way of helping to pay for the costs of the wedding and honeymoon. (see p.64 Gifts for Special Occasions)

Q How much money should I give as a gift?

A That depends on how close you are to the person getting married, but in general if it's a friend, you'll give about 20,000 to 30,000 yen. You can ask other people you know who are going to the wedding how much they are giving.

Recently, some wedding receptions are parties thrown by friends. In this case, the guests all contribute to the cost of the reception. If you are invited to this kind of reception, the invitation will state clearly how much it costs to attend and you will pay the fee when you arrive. You don't have to give any other money in addition to this as a wedding present.

Q Where do I give my gift money?

A You will give it at the reception table. First you'll sign your name in a book. Then you will pass the envelope with both hands to the person at the reception table.

Q Are weddings held on any day of the year?

A Weddings can be held on any day, but most people refer to a traditional calendar that dictates which days are luckiest. These days are called *taian*, and the *taian* that fall on weekends tend to be in the most demand and therefore the most difficult to reserve.

Q How much do weddings cost?

A Getting married in Japan takes a lot of money. According to one survey, weddings and receptions at hotels cost an average of 3.5 million yen.

Adding to this the cost of the betrothal gifts, the honeymoon, and money for furniture and other things needed to set up a new married life, the average becomes 7.3 million yen!

Q Why does the bride keep changing her clothes?

A This is known as *oironaoshi*. Many brides want to have a chance to wear a kimono, a white wedding dress, as well as at least one formal party dress. In order to do so, the bride will leave the reception, change, and come back several times. Each time she returns, the master of ceremonies will announce her arrival and it is customary to ooh and ah.

Q What is the big shopping bag that is distributed as the guests leave?

A It contains various gifts for the guests, called *hikidemono*. It is a way of thanking the guests for coming and the gifts also serve as a souvenir of the wedding. In some places in Japan the presents are so numerous that the bags are quite heavy. Recently, guests are sometimes given catalogues from which they may choose the gift that they want.

Age-Related Events

What years in life are special?

shichi-go-san

It's November and recently Patrick Short has noticed a lot of children wearing kimono walking down the street accompanied by their parents, especially on the weekends. He wonders where they are going and if there is some special event for children at this time of year.

Seven, five, three

The children Patrick saw were no doubt celebrating *Shichi-go-san*. **Shichi-go-san means seven, five, three. It is an event on November 15 dating back to the Edo period (17th century) for girls age three and seven, and three- and five-year-old boys.**

This is a big deal for children. Traditionally girls wore special kimono and boys wore *hakama* trousers. Nowadays some wear Western clothes instead. Some people buy the clothes but renting is also popular. Many girls additionally go to beauty parlors to have their hair and faces elaborately made up.

On weekends around November 15 many dressed-up children can be seen

with their parents. They go to a Shinto shrine to give thanks for their growth so far and to pray for their future health.

The children are given *chitose ame*, "one-thousand-year-candy," a long thin stick of hard candy that is supposed to represent wishes for a long life. After visiting the shrine many children have their pictures taken by professional photographers and go somewhere to have a special meal with their family.

Becoming adult at 20

People are recognized as adults at 20 in Japan and gain the right to vote, drink alcohol and smoke cigarettes. While each person acquires these privileges on their own 20th birthday, all those who are 20 on the second Monday of January celebrate their coming of age together. This is a national holiday.

Many 20-year-old women wear gorgeous long-sleeved kimono, called *furisode*. Long sleeves on a kimono indicate the woman is still unmarried. Married women do not wear *furisode*, rather they have short-sleeved kimono, so many young women rent a kimono rather than buying one. 20-year-old men usually wear suits. Regional civic halls hold special events, after which most of the new adults spend the day enjoying their maturity in various ways.

Photographer shops are extremely crowded on Coming-of-Age Day so many women dress up in their kimono to be photographed sometime in advance of the actual day.

One full cycle at 60

When a person becomes 60 they have completed a full cycle of the zodiac signs. This is called *kanreki*. Because they've finished one full cycle, **the 60th birthday traditionally signifies the onset of old age and the return to babyhood.** Until quite recently 60 has been the standard age for retirement.

Kanreki is celebrated with a party and presents. **The new 60-year-old often wears red and/or is given a red cushion by their children.** This is a symbol that he or she has become a baby once more and the color red is also supposed to ward off evil. The 70th, 77th, 80th, 88th and 90th birthdays are also considered special and celebratory parties are held.

G o o d *to* k n o w ·····························

- ●せいじんしき ［*seijin-shiki*］
- ●ふりそで ［*furisode*］
- ●いんきょ ［*inkyo*］
- ●きねんしゃしん ［*kinen shashin*］
- ●せいじん・おとな ［*seijin/otona*］
- ●おいわい ［*oiwai*］
- ●ちゃんちゃんこ ［*chanchanko*］

- ▷ a Coming-of-Age ceremony
- ▷ a long-sleeved kimono for unmarried women
- ▷ a retired person
- ▷ a commemorative photo
- ▷ an adult
- ▷ a celebration or a present to celebrate an event
- ▷ a vest (Traditionally someone who became 60 was given a red vest.)

New Year's

Out with the old, in with the new

How to pray at a shrine

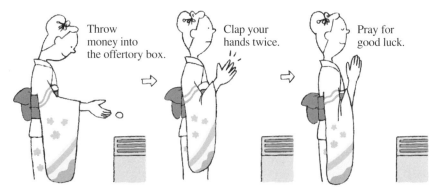

Throw money into the offertory box.

Clap your hands twice.

Pray for good luck.

Rebecca Fish watched Christmas come and go fairly quietly in Japan. But as the end of the year drew closer she sensed a feeling of anticipation among her Japanese colleagues. They had looked forward to other holidays as time off from work, but their expectation now seemed stronger than at any other time of the year. Rebecca wondered what exactly went on at New Year's in Japan.

Busy times at year-end

December in Japan is known as *shiwasu* which literally means "teachers running around," the idea being that even teachers who are normally very dignified end up scurrying about to get things done before the new year. In the midst of all this productive action businesspeople also frequently go out to *bōnen-kai*, or "forgetting the year" parties. The parties don't stop after the new year begins, but the name changes to *shinnen-kai*, "new year parties."

One reason for the hustle is that most offices close a few days before the end of December and stay closed for about the first three or four days of January. **After tying up loose ends at work and clean-ing up the office, businesspeople return to their homes and participate in major year-end housecleaning.** All the windows are washed, grime is removed from kitchen fans, and ladders are brought out to scrub hard-to-reach areas. It is important to Japanese people to greet the new year with a feeling of purity.

When everything is spick and span, special new year's decorations are put up and special new year's food, *osechi-ryōri*, is prepared. On New Year's Eve people typically eat *toshikoshi soba*, long buckwheat noodles said to bring good health and a long life, watch a popular singing contest on TV and go out late at night to ring in the new year by hitting the gongs at Buddhist temples 108 times.

Quiet first day

Nobody is supposed to work, cook or clean the house on New Year's Day. Traditionally *osechi-ryōri* was eaten for three days. In addition, people eat a special soup with rice cakes called *ozōni* and in the morning adults toast the new year with specially flavored Japanese sake, *otoso*.

Besides eating and drinking, three other activities take place on New Year's Day. First, children are given New Year's money, *otoshidama*, in little envelopes. Next, people read the New Year's cards, *nenga-jō*, delivered precisely on the 1st. Third, people get ready to make their first visit of the year to a Shinto shrine or Buddhist temple, *hatsumōde*. Many women wear beautiful kimono.

At the shrine

Large shrines are unbelievably crowded. **The Meiji Shrine in Tokyo sees more than three million visitors in the first three days of the new year and there are about 88.5 million visitors to various shrines during this period.**

People shuffle along in line and when they get to the front of the shrine they make offerings of any amount of money and pray for a happy new year. After that, they often buy decorative arrows, *hamaya*, to ward off evil, which they display in their homes for the year and buy fortunes, called *omikuji*.

The fortunes are written on white strips of paper and indicate your chances for happiness and success in various realms of your life — health, business, and romance. Then it's back home to enjoy a little more New Year's food and sake.

G o o d *to* **k n o w** ·····································

● よいおとしをおむかえください。
　 [*Yoi otoshi o omukae kudasai.*]

▷ Please have a happy new year. (said before Jan. 1st)

● あけましておめでとうございます。
　 [*Akemashite omedetō gozaimasu.*]

▷ Happy new year! (said on, and after, Jan. 1st)

● かどまつ [*kadomatsu*]

▷ pine decorations placed in front of the house

● かがみもち [*kagami mochi*]

▷ two round rice cakes, one on top of the other, used as a room decoration

● おとしだま [*otoshidama*]

▷ New Year's money for children

● はつもうで [*hatsumōde*]

▷ the first visit of the year to a shrine or temple

● おみくじ [*omikuji*]

▷ a fortune

Death

How do Japanese people observe the ending of life?

Near Sally Porter's home there is a small graveyard and she sometimes sees families visit it bringing flowers or incense. She has also seen the Buddhist family altars in some people's homes with pictures of deceased relatives. She'd like to know more about how death is observed in Japan.

The Buddhist wake and funeral

90% of wakes and funerals in Japan are Buddhist and the rest are Shinto or Christian. When a person passes away, those who knew him or her are notified of the days and times of the wake, *otsuya*, and funeral, *osōshiki/kokubetsu-shiki*. Family members and very close friends will attend both.

Usually other people go just to the funeral, although if you can't make it to the funeral because of a schedule conflict you can go to the wake instead. If you can't go to either you can send an obituary gift of money, a telegram or flowers. Wakes and funerals may be held at homes, temples or funeral halls.

Traditionally people stayed up all night at wakes but these days wakes are only a few hours long. **At both wakes and funerals those attending sign their names as they arrive and make an obituary gift of money in a special envelope, called a *kōden-bukuro*.**

A Buddhist priest will chant some prayers and those attending will burn incense. A light meal is also served at the wake. At the funeral, in addition to the prayers and incense burning, there will be speeches and reading of telegrams. It is customary to go up to the casket and say goodbye at this time.

Cremation

Following the funeral, those attending will see off family members and very close friends going to the crematorium. **Burial is extremely rare.** At the crematorium, those present will watch the casket enter the flames, then wait while the corpse is cremated.

After cremation, those present will stand around the smoldering remains. Two people will pick up a piece of bone together with special chopsticks, put it into an urn, and pass the chopsticks onto the next pair.

Because the bones are picked up at the same time by two sets of chopsticks at a cremation, it is taboo to touch food in this way when eating. Japanese people will put food on a plate for the other person to pick up, rather than passing it directly from one set of chopsticks to the other. After the ceremony the bones are kept at a temple or cemetery.

Remembering the deceased

After death, the Buddhist priest gives the deceased a new Buddhist name, called a *kaimyō*, and a wooden tablet called an *ihai* is made with the name on it. The *ihai* is placed in the family Buddhist altar. Many people light incense and place a bowl of rice in front of the Buddhist altar every day.

Those close to the deceased will further attend memorial services seven days, 49 days, and one year after the death. **Families additionally visit the graves of deceased relatives during the Bon season in August and/or in March or September during the vernal or autumnal equinox.** Other memorial services are held by relatives at three years, seven years, 13 years and may continue further.

G o o d *to* k n o w ·····································

● ごしゅうしょうさまです。 [*Goshūshō-sama desu.*]   ▷ Please accept my condolences.

● ちからをおとさずに。 [*Chikara o otosazu ni.*]   ▷ Please keep up your courage.

● なくなる [*nakunaru*]   ▷ pass away

● こじん [*kojin*]   ▷ the deceased

● おつや [*otsuya*]   ▷ a wake

● おそうしき・こくべつしき [*osōshiki/kokubetsu-shiki*]   ▷ a funeral service

● こうでん [*kōden*]   ▷ an obituary gift of money

● おせんこうをあげる [*osenkō o ageru*]   ▷ burn incense

● かそう [*kasō*]   ▷ cremation

● おはか [*ohaka*]   ▷ a grave

● ぶつだん [*butsudan*]   ▷ a family Buddhist altar

Funeral Q&A

How do I pay my last respects?

How to burn incense

Doug Bradley heard from a colleague that a person from a related company has passed away. A few years earlier Doug had worked closely with the man and he feels that he'd like to pay his last respects. However, Doug realizes that he knows very little about what goes on at funerals in Japan.

Q How much money should I bring or send as an obituary gift?

A It depends on your relationship to the deceased, but 5,000 to 10,000 yen is pretty standard. You place the money in a special envelope, called a *kōden-bukuro,* which you can buy at stationery or convenience stores. You will later receive a present in return from the deceased's family such as small towels or green tea.

Q I can't go to the funeral. How do I send a telegram?

A There is a special type of telegram for funeral condolences, called a *chōden*, in Japan. You can make the arrangements at NTT (telephone company). You can also send flowers to the place the funeral will be held, or send money to the deceased's family. You can ask a Japanese acquaintance to help you with the arrangements.

Q What should I wear to a wake or funeral?

A Traditionally people wear a black kimono with their family crest on it. However, most people now wear Western clothes. Men wear a black suit and black tie with a white shirt. Women wear a black dress or suit. The only accessory that is considered appropriate for women is a pearl necklace.

Q Are there any days that are inauspicious for funerals?

A According to the traditional calendar, some days are *tomobiki*. *Tomobiki* literally means pulling your friend and it is believed that if you have a funeral on this type of day another death will soon follow. Therefore, these days are avoided.

Q How do I burn the incense?

A While the Buddhist priest is chanting prayers for the deceased, people go up to the front, one by one, beginning with the family and close friends. Here's how it's done (see illustrations):
❶ Stand in front of the Buddhist altar and bow to the picture of the deceased.
❷ Take a pinch of powdered incense, raise it up in front of your face, then sprinkle it on the incense that is already burning.
❸ Place your palms together and pray for the deceased.
It is believed that the fragrance of the incense purifies the spirit of the dead person. Basically, you can copy what the person in front of you does.

Q Why do people eat light food and drink alcohol after the wake?

A While eating, the bereaved and the guests reminisce about the person who has passed away. It is thought that by doing so, the soul of the departed will be consoled. The food is also a way of thanking the guests for coming. Alcohol is thought to cleanse those attending of the impurity of death.

Q As I was leaving the funeral I received a packet of salt. What's that for?

A As noted in the above question, it is thought that death is impure. Salt is believed to purify or protect from bad things. When people return from wakes or funerals they sprinkle a bit of salt on their bodies before entering their houses in order to purify themselves.

Q Why do people receive a new name, *kaimyō*, after death?

A According to Buddhism, after death people become disciples of Buddha. There are various ranks to these names depending on the price you pay to the Buddhist priest who bestows the name. The system varies depending on the Buddhist sect.

Q What about Christian funerals in Japan?

A The main ceremony is similar to that of Christian funerals in the West. One particularly Japanese custom is that of *kenka*. A flower is handed out to each person attending the funeral. These flowers are laid on the altar. Be sure that your flower faces the same direction as everyone else's.

Other Beginnings and Endings

How important are entrance ceremonies?

nyūgaku   sotsugyō

Rick Carlson's colleague, Shinsuke Mori, has a daughter who is about to start first grade. Rick was surprised to find out that both Mori-*san* and his wife, who also works full-time, would be taking a day off work to attend their daughter's entrance ceremony. He wondered how important starting elementary school was in Japan.

Making a ceremony of it

Japan loves making a ceremony of beginnings and endings. There are formal entrance ceremonies and graduation ceremonies at the beginning and end of elementary school, junior high school and high school. Schoolchildren additionally attend smaller ceremonies marking the beginning and ending of each school term from first grade through 12th. This adds up to a total of 36 school ceremonies in 12 years.

When people are accepted as company employees they also take part in a *naitei-shiki*, a ceremony confirming their employment. When they actually join the company they will attend another entrance ceremony, *nyūsha-shiki*. On top of this, many companies hold ceremonies at the beginning of each new year.

All's well that begins well

There is far more emphasis on beginnings than on endings. Things must be begun properly and with due pomp. Starting at a new school is considered very important. No Japanese person would be surprised that Mr. and Mrs. Mori were taking off work for their daughter's entrance ceremony; they'd be more surprised if the Moris didn't go.

Almost all parents attend their children's entrance ceremonies for elementary school, junior high school and high school. Some additionally attend college entrance ceremonies although by this time the children are seen as independent adults.

Both the parents and the children dress up for these occasions. Usually the principal gives a speech and a group photograph is taken. The school band may perform a concert. The whole thing takes a couple of hours. Official schoolwork begins the following day.

Graduations less important

People graduate in March and start a new school or new job in April. Starting about February, department stores will have signs up suggesting that certain items would make great gifts for people starting new schools or companies. There are many fewer signs making appeals for graduation gifts.

Perhaps because it is harder in Japan to get into a school or company than it is to finish, graduations are less of a big deal. Parents are also less likely to attend their children's graduations.

Nonetheless, in March many Japanese women wear beautiful kimono, *hakama* trousers or nice dresses on their college graduation days. In the Meiji and Taisho periods, female university students wore *hakama* regularly. When women wear them now for graduation it is a nostalgic reminder of former days. Men usually wear suits. Western caps and gowns are rare.

Following the graduation ceremony the students usually give a party for their teachers, called a *shaon-kai*, to thank them for their instruction. And then it's on to the next beginning.

G o o d *to* k n o w ....

- ●にゅうがく [*nyūgaku*]　　　　　▷ entering a school
- ●そつぎょう [*sotsugyō*]　　　　　▷ graduation
- ●にゅうがくしき [*nyūgaku-shiki*]　　▷ a school entrance ceremony
- ●にゅうしゃしき [*nyūsha-shiki*]　　▷ a company entrance ceremony
- ●そつぎょうしき [*sotsugyō-shiki*]　　▷ a graduation ceremony
- ●そつぎょうしょうしょ [*sotsugyō shōsho*]　▷ a graduation diploma
- ●しぎょうしき [*shigyō-shiki*]　　▷ a beginning-of-term ceremony
- ●しゅうぎょうしき [*shūgyō-shiki*]　　▷ an end-of-term ceremony
- ●しんにゅうせい [*shinnyūsei*]　　▷ a new student
- ●そつぎょうせい [*sotsugyōsei*]　　▷ a graduate
- ●しんそつ [*shinsotsu*]　　　　　▷ a new college graduate
- ●しんにゅうしゃいん [*shinnyū-shain*]　▷ a new company employee

● What's going on?

Distance from Japanese colleagues ···p.10 Inside and Outside/
p.56 Getting Along with Friends

Feelings of isolation ·······································p.12 Group Harmony/p.28 Bullying

Work not valued ···p.48 Complimenting

Troubled relationship with boss ·····························p.16 Shame/p.54 Age Differences

Confusion about yes and no ·····································p.18 Inference/p.20 Ambiguity

Lack of straightforwardness ·····························p.14 Real Intentions and Stated Principles/
p.18 Inference/p.20 Ambiguity/p.32 Modesty

Too-friendly behavior ·······························p.26 Consideration for Others

Suppressing frustration ···p.24 Perseverance

Working late ···p.22 Diligence

Strange gestures ···································p.42 Nonverbal Communication

Puzzling topic openers ·························p.50 Invitations/p.52 Requests

● Gaining deeper relationships

Learning some Japanese phrases··············p.38 Hellos and Goodbyes/p.44 Expressing Gratitude/
p.46 Apologizing/p.74 Really, Really, Good to Know

Building trust ··p.30 Moral Obligation

Socializing away from the office·············p.56 Getting Along with Friends/p.60 Going Out to Eat/
p.72 Going Out Drinking

Taking advantage of Japanese customs ················p.62 Gift-Giving Seasons/p.66 Greeting Cards

● Necessary etiquette

Basic business manners ································p.36 Meeting Someone for the First Time/
p.40 What to Call People

Guest dos and don'ts ······················p.68 Visiting Others' Homes/p.70 Eating at Others' Homes

Seniority issues ···p.54 Age Differences

Neighborly ways ·····························p.18 Inference/p.58 Getting Along with Neighbors

How-tos for important events ···············p.64 Gifts for Special Occasions/p.82 Wedding Q&A/
p.90 Funeral Q&A

Hiragana/Katakana/Rōmaji

あ	い	う	え	お
ア	イ	ウ	エ	オ
a	i	u	e	o
か	き	く	け	こ
カ	キ	ク	ケ	コ
ka	ki	ku	ke	ko
さ	し	す	せ	そ
サ	シ	ス	セ	ソ
sa	shi	su	se	so
た	ち	つ	て	と
タ	チ	ツ	テ	ト
ta	chi	tsu	te	to
な	に	ぬ	ね	の
ナ	ニ	ヌ	ネ	ノ
na	ni	nu	ne	no
は	ひ	ふ	へ	ほ
ハ	ヒ	フ	ヘ	ホ
ha	hi	fu	he	ho
ま	み	む	め	も
マ	ミ	ム	メ	モ
ma	mi	mu	me	mo
や	(い)	ゆ	(え)	よ
ヤ	(イ)	ユ	(エ)	ヨ
ya	(i)	yu	(e)	yo
ら	り	る	れ	ろ
ラ	リ	ル	レ	ロ
ra	ri	ru	re	ro
わ	(い)	(う)	(え)	を
ワ	(イ)	(ウ)	(エ)	ヲ
wa	(i)	(u)	(e)	o
ん				
ン				
n				

が	ぎ	ぐ	げ	ご
ガ	ギ	グ	ゲ	ゴ
ga	gi	gu	ge	go
ざ	じ	ず	ぜ	ぞ
ザ	ジ	ズ	ゼ	ゾ
za	ji	zu	ze	zo
だ	ぢ	づ	で	ど
ダ	ヂ	ヅ	デ	ド
da	ji	zu	de	do
ば	び	ぶ	べ	ぼ
バ	ビ	ブ	ベ	ボ
ba	bi	bu	be	bo
ぱ	ぴ	ぷ	ぺ	ぽ
パ	ピ	プ	ペ	ポ
pa	pi	pu	pe	po

きゃ	きゅ	きょ	りゃ	りゅ	りょ
キャ	キュ	キョ	リャ	リュ	リョ
kya	kyu	kyo	rya	ryu	ryo
しゃ	しゅ	しょ	ぎゃ	ぎゅ	ぎょ
シャ	シュ	ショ	ギャ	ギュ	ギョ
sha	shu	sho	gya	gyu	gyo
ちゃ	ちゅ	ちょ	じゃ	じゅ	じょ
チャ	チュ	チョ	ジャ	ジュ	ジョ
cha	chu	cho	ja	ju	jo
にゃ	にゅ	にょ	びゃ	びゅ	びょ
ニャ	ニュ	ニョ	ビャ	ビュ	ビョ
nya	nyu	nyo	bya	byu	byo
ひゃ	ひゅ	ひょ	ぴゃ	ぴゅ	ぴょ
ヒャ	ヒュ	ヒョ	ピャ	ピュ	ピョ
hya	hyu	hyo	pya	pyu	pyo
みゃ	みゅ	みょ			
ミャ	ミュ	ミョ			
mya	myu	myo			

Kate Elwood has lived in Japan for 18 years and is a fluent speaker of Japanese. She has worked in the areas of international public relations and journalism and is a full-time lecturer in the junior college division of Sagami Women's University in Kanagawa, Japan, where she teaches various intercultural communication courses. Elwood has also appeared on a number of programs on Japanese public television teaching English language and American culture to Japanese viewers. From April 2000 to March 2001 she wrote a 12-part series for the NHK (National Broadcasting Corp.) monthly textbook *English Business World* called "Say What You Mean," focusing on cross-cultural misunderstanding.